AF230433

Grief, Hope, Baseball

Essays

Published by St. Petersburg Press
St. Petersburg, FL
www.stpetersburgpress.com

Design and composition by St. Petersburg Press
Cover design by St. Petersburg Press and Isa Crosta
Author photo by Chanel Fernandez
Graffiti art by Jose Flores

Print ISBN: 978-1-964239-41-5
eBook ISBN: 978-1-964239-42-2
Library of Congress Control Number: 2026902369

First Edition

GRIEF, HOPE, BASEBALL

Essays

By Jessica Rios, LCSW-R

Foreword by

Cynthia Santiago-Borbon, LCSW-R

Table of Contents

To my nieces, nephews, and God children, may you always find strength in your roots, believe in yourselves, and feel inspired to chase your dreams and reach your full potential. If you ever need reminding, know that I got you and love you all so much.

For my clients, whom I am honored to walk alongside and to be trusted by, and for all the grievers who continue to find joy and hope every day despite the daily challenges of losing those you love.

FOREWORD

Grief, Hope, and Baseball - at first glance, these may seem like an unusual trio. But as you hold this book in your hands, you're about to embark on a journey where these elements intertwine in profound and unexpected ways. This book, written with depth, authenticity, and heart, explores the universal experience of loss and the enduring power of hope, all through the lens of America's favorite pastime.

When Jessica first shared the concept of this book with me, I was immediately struck by its uniqueness. As someone who has experienced grief in my own life, I know the ache of loss and the search for meaning that follows. Baseball, with its rhythms, rituals, and strength, offers a surprising yet fitting metaphor for navigating life's challenges. It's a game of endurance, strategy, and perseverance. Qualities we draw upon when faced with life's most difficult moments.

I remember a moment in my own life when grief seemed insurmountable. It was during a quiet afternoon sitting by the ocean that I found an unexpected sense of peace. For many, like Jessica, solace can be found in the world of sports. Even if baseball isn't your typical passion, Jessica's exploration of baseball as a metaphor reminds us that persistence and fortitude are essential, both on the field and in our personal journeys through hardship and healing.

Jessica brings an unparalleled perspective to this narrative, not only as a talented writer but also as a skilled psychotherapist, death doula, and coach who has dedicated her career to helping others navigate the complexities of grief. Her professional insights, combined with her personal connection to the themes of grief and hope, make this book a powerful resource for anyone seeking healing and inspiration. Whether you're a baseball fan or simply someone seeking solace and meaning, the stories and insights shared here will resonate deeply.

As Jessica's life coach for many years, I have witnessed her profound commitment to her clients and her work. She approaches every endeavor, whether in therapy, coaching sessions, or writing with compassion, wisdom, and an unwavering belief in the transformative power of hope. This book is a reflection of that dedication, and I'm honored to have played a small role in supporting her journey.

As you turn these pages, prepare to laugh, cry, and reflect. Jessica has created something truly special. A tribute to the fortitude of the human spirit and the hope that sustains us. It's a book that will leave an indelible mark on your heart and remind you that, no matter the curveballs life throws, there is always a way forward.

To Jessica, thank you for sharing your story, your expertise, and your wisdom. To you, the reader, thank you for taking this journey. May this book bring you comfort, inspiration, and perhaps even a new appreciation for the game of baseball.

Cynthia Santiago-Borbon, LCSW-R

IN THE BOX

The batter's box is where a hitter stands alone, anticipating what's coming.

*I*t is the bottom of the ninth inning with two outs, a full count, and the game is tied.

My sister calls my cell phone. She is in hysteria, telling me I need to get to her home ASAP because she had to call EMS for our father. I know something is wrong. It's in the tone of her voice. I don't question it.

The batter is walking up to the plate.

My partner drives me to her home. There is no way I can drive in the Bronx knowing something is wrong.

Adrenaline is pumping and the batter takes his stance.

I'm so nervous and sit in silence in the passenger seat.

The batter observes the strength of the pitcher.

I get to her building and enter the lobby. I'm not allowed to go into the apartment. "They're working on him," someone says. My initial thought is, *Who the fuck are you?* But it quickly fades away. Anger never lasts long for me.

The batter keeps his eye on the ball.

I stay calm. I stare steadily at the door. *Where's my nephew? Where are my sisters?* My mom is on her way. *What happened?* Stay focused for when that door opens. That's all I keep telling myself. Stay calm.

He sees the ball coming closer and digs in because he knows this is it.

FDNY is here. In my experience, I've only seen the fire department arrive for a medical call when the person is deceased.

This is the moment he knew was coming.

My dad, Moncho, is dead. He *has* to be if FDNY is here.

He has the chance to win the game. He swings at the ball.

My sister comes out and is crying and yelling. She keeps saying that she tried to help him breathe. He called for help. She called 911 immediately. She gave him CPR.

The batter can feel the intensity of the ball making contact on that perfect spot of the bat.

I can hear footsteps nearing the door of their apartment. I hear the doorknob turning, the sound of metal and squeaky hinges as the door opens.

The batter can hear the sweet sound of the crack. It's sharp and the sound echoes throughout the stadium.

The stretcher wheels move with muted cadence and the floor echoes with a somber farewell.

The batter drops the bat because he is confident the resounding smack of the ball is a home run.

Moncho is on this stretcher. Moncho is not breathing. He is wearing an oxygen mask, but he isn't breathing.

The crowd is cheering.

We're all just standing in the lobby. I'm staring over at my mother and sister on the other side of the stretcher. They are wailing.

It is an explosion of unrestrained joy.

Relief unexpectedly washes over me. I don't *want* Moncho to die. I just don't want him to keep struggling, either.

The sound of the home run echoes.

Each wail is an expression of pain, a symphony of sorrow that echoes the depth of Moncho's loss. Then, we get to the hospital alongside EMS and FDNY.

Fans are hugging each other in excitement and giving high fives to complete strangers.

The sound of everyone's cries hangs heavy, carrying with it the weight of shared sorrow and anguish. We hug each other, seeking comfort, but there isn't any.

Victory!

We wait for word from doctors regarding Moncho's health.

The game is over.

The doctors have confirmed that Moncho has died. We stand in the exam room where we cried. I stroke his feet and legs, taking in the fact that my dad will no longer take another breath in this world.

Time for the fans to commute back home.

When we leave the hospital, it's dark out. I can't tell you what time it is. My grandmother, aunt, and cousin are out there for support. They hug us and my grandmother prays. She always prays.

Many of them walk to the train station after the game.

I walked back to my sister's home. To where my father took his last breath.

They even have a little pep in their steps while they smile and reflect on the nine innings and that game-winning home run.

I reflect on Moncho's life. I reflect on his struggles and his victories. I reflect on our relationship and its meaning.

It's 2009. My father is dead. I'm relieved. This wasn't the first time he was taken away.

ON THE SHELF

When a player gets hurt or misses time, he is "shelved" or "on the shelf."

My stomach twists into knots as I watch the scene unfold in our living room. The grown-ups' faces blur together through my tears. I'm scared, but I don't understand why everyone is crying.

When it happens, Mom's wails echo through our apartment while my sister leans over the banister. Her cries for Moncho blend into the chaos around us. Everything feels loud.

A neighbor rushes over and cradles my mother, rubbing her back and whispering things I can't hear. Their adult daughter, a familiar face, turns her attention toward me.

"Want to play with your toys?" she asks gently, trying to distract me from whatever is happening.

I nod, even though I want to understand what's going on. All I know for sure is that officers are taking away Moncho. His presence in our lives has been erratic. Sometimes he's there, sometimes he isn't, so I wonder when he will return.

I feel sad for a moment because everyone around me is sad, but I can't understand why this time feels different. I feel stuck in the on-deck circle of my emotions, practicing swings and never getting an at bat.

Is this permanent? Is Moncho going to be gone for good? These are the thoughts running through my mind, but only for a short time. My attention shifts to the toy in my hands.

I continue to play with my neighbor. I hug my stuffed animal extra tight, promising to be the best kid ever if it will bring Moncho back home.

When we are young, we don't understand time. Days feel

like weeks, and weeks feel like forever.

I miss Moncho. He's different when he's with us. He is patient and playful, showering my sister and me with attention. I yearn for the times we all cuddle together on the couch to watch WWE, sharing the excitement of Hulk Hogan and the Undertaker. My sister and I lie on our bedsheets covered with wrestling heroes, talking about our favorite matches and waiting for Moncho to come watch with us.

One day, Mom sits us down on the couch. "Moncho is in prison," she explains, her voice cracking.

I know that means he's done something wrong, something called a crime, but no one says anything about what crime. And I don't ask. I'm growing up in the era of "You're a child. You don't ask questions, you stay in a child's place, and you don't listen to adult conversations."

I'm learning to keep my voice and feelings pushed down deep inside, where they stay hidden and unexpressed. We have very little say in anything, and asking questions or sharing our emotions means we're being disrespectful.

A few weeks later, Mom decides we are going to visit Moncho.

On the bus with my mother and sister, I watch the anxious and distressed expressions on the faces of adults, mostly females dressed in nicely ironed outfits. I press my face against the window, watching the city change as we get farther from home.

When we arrive, we are met with a large display of guards and other security measures. Officers with guns and dogs are everywhere we turn. But my excitement and love for Moncho is stronger than any fear of being in this place.

My sister's face radiates with joy as we walk through the detectors and checkpoints. The crinkle of paper in my pocket reminds me of the card I eagerly crafted for my dad, pouring my love into every stroke of the pencil and crayons I used.

We are taken to a room full of solid, white circular tables. I look down and notice the tables are bolted to the floor.

Nothing in this room feels wrong to me. It is all…normal, and I feel appreciative of this moment.

Then I see him. Moncho is sitting at one of the tables, smiling and holding back tears when he spots us. Once we're at the table with him, my body feels warm, my palms are sweating, and my heart is racing as I prepare to show my creation to my dad. I am eager to share this token of affection with him.

I pull on my dad's arm, "Dad. Dad."

"I'm speaking with Mom. Please wait until we finish. Don't forget to say, 'excuse me,'" he says assertively. He isn't mean about it, so why do I feel so sad? I nod, tucking the card away in my pocket.

I'll wait, I decide.

He finishes the conversation with my mother and turns to me with big eyes and curiosity. *I should mention the card*, I think. *But maybe I should just forget it.* I feel an immense sense of rejection. I decide I'm going to talk to my dad for as long as I can. We talk about school, wrestling, gifts, and so much more.

Later, on the bus, Mom tells me the conversation I interrupted between my parents was about her ending things with Moncho. She has met someone (my future stepfather), and she wants to live a healthier life with him.

When we get home, I crumple up the card and throw it in the trash. Dad will be released eventually, I think, and I'll have other things to share with him then.

Moncho's time in jail is temporary, and I'm filled with hope that I will see him again, soon. Even though I don't know exactly when. Even baseball players on the injured list know their return date. But I am playing a game with no scoreboard to track until Moncho's return.

Yet, I lean into hope. The reassurance I feel that this separation is temporary becomes my anchor. It holds me in place, in a place where I don't have to be sad that he isn't around right now, in a place where I *hope* that he will be released. Soon.

Two Christmases pass without Moncho.

For one of those two Christmases, we get an abundance of

gifts from strangers. Moncho sold drugs, but this one Christmas is unforgettable because it is more than we have ever had, even when Moncho was hustling on the streets and making *money*. The gifts are an extravagant collection primarily comprised of Barbie stuff.

It is way too much for me: Barbies, Kens, a Barbie Ferrari, an entire wardrobe, a closet, pets, and so much more. My younger sister loves it. We overhear that strangers volunteered to buy presents for children whose parents are in jail.

My older sister and I love the GI Joe and soldier toys, particularly those that scurry across the floor. We walk through Delancey Street with our mom and stepdad. I get distracted watching the soldiers crawl on the side of the street beside the swimming electronic fish in a water-filled urinal bedpan. I can relate to GI Joe, but not Barbie. No offense if you are a Barbie enthusiast.

Maybe it's because GI Joe represents strength and protection, like our father does when he's present. I want to be that strength and protection for my family since I don't know when Moncho will return.

Instead of telling anyone how nervous I feel, I decide not to cause extra stress by crying or complaining.

The soldier toys become symbols of hope for me – proof that Moncho is being strong while he's away. They also become a safe place for all the emotions I'm not allowed to share and have to keep in: Fear. Shame. Doubt. Nervousness.

The hardest part isn't missing Moncho. It's hearing what other people say about him.

Adults who think we children aren't paying attention whisper (and sometimes they *don't* whisper), casting judgment on my father.

Family members, neighbors, and even parents of friends talk badly about Moncho, and each word feels like an assault. I want desperately to defend him, to shout that my dad, despite his choices, wouldn't willingly choose to be separated from his daughters.

But in my family, kids do not check adults when they speak. Naturally, I keep my thoughts and feelings inside, and I focus on gratitude. My go-to emotion because it is the only one allowed.

…at least we have a home

…at least my mom isn't getting hit

…at least my stepfather is in the picture

I make a mental list of things to be grateful for:

My family, friends, music, pencils, crayons, paper, books, parents, and so much more!

But when I'm alone, I feel other feelings too:

Irritated, frustrated, hurt, angry, sad, stupid, lonely, bored, tired, scared, confused, insignificant, embarrassed.

Mostly, I feel shame because I take in these judgments and have nowhere to put my feelings.

Family members say we won't make much of ourselves because of our parents' decisions. No one seems to recognize the burden I'm carrying. I lock my emotions away, allowing the shame to grow in the dark spaces inside me.

And yet, there is a flicker of hope. This separation is temporary. I cling to the idea that my dad will be released from prison and will show everyone that he can change.

That he loves us! He loves me!

Like in baseball, I keep hoping for a comeback. But sometimes, even when players come back from being hurt, things aren't the same as before.

RELIEVERS

**A reliever (a pitcher) comes into the game
at a dire time to hold the
other team at bay or preserve a victory.**

I see a needle in the shoe rack behind the door. My heart races as I think about where I'm going to put this so my sisters won't see it and accidently cut themselves.

An adult hasn't really confirmed that this is a drug, but I know that when it gets used, adults tend to enter another dimension of daydreaming, crying, yelling, and so many seemingly intense emotions, or none at all.

When we walk with Mom through the streets of LES (Lower East Side), specifically through Tompkins Square Park, we see people shooting up all the time. I'm never scared, just cautious. We walk quickly through that park. Living in NYC, a quick walk usually means we have somewhere to go, which is most of the time. We are always cautious because we don't want to be involved in any dangerous situations.

There are many times I pretend to be asleep while Moncho is using drugs in our home. Under the sheets, my heart pounds like a batter practicing endless swings in the cages. I feel this weird sense of distance during these nights. Distance because I don't recognize my father when he is high. He becomes aggressive, and that scares and confuses me. I squeeze my eyes shut, praying like a fan in the ninth inning of a losing game that tomorrow will bring back my *real* dad, the *loving* Moncho who makes me feel loved, nurtured, and important.

But right now, I need to deal with this needle.

I feel responsible for my sisters, even though I'm the middle child. I don't want them exposed to this, so I often move needles I find to places where adults will see them and "hide" them better.

Mom is in the kitchen, so I decide to try and quickly place it on the table where she'll notice it. My hands are trembling, and my chest feels tight. I look over at the needle in the shoe rack and measure the distance between it and the kitchen table. I glance at Mom, who is cooking while putting clothes away.

How quickly can I do this without Mom noticing that I touched it? Without her realizing that she left this needle there in the first place. My sisters are playing together, and they aren't looking at me. Normally, I'd want their attention. Not today. *Don't look at what I'm about to do.*

I take a deep breath, slowly walk in front of the shoe rack, and grab the needle. I check to make sure my sisters are still ignoring me. After taking another peek at Mami, who is stirring the rice while holding the caldero, I quickly put the needle on the edge of the table and slide down to the floor where my sisters are playing.

They look at me, annoyed that I've interrupted their game. I chuckle nervously.

Mom walks past the table and sees *it*. She gasps, grabs it, and looks our way, clutching it to her chest. I pretend I don't see her looking at us.

She hides it somewhere. I don't know where because I look away from what she is doing. She seems relieved.

I am always thankful for my mom in these moments, but I wish I didn't have to be so careful all the time. I am the family's relief pitcher, always warming up, ready to protect my sisters from danger.

Our home on East Sixth Street faces the Sixth Street Community Center, a haven where my sisters, cousins, and friends spend many days, especially during the summer months. The building is an old tenement with wooden steps, and I feel so eager and excited every time I get to go outside and play with everyone there.

The recreation staff and the Police Athletic League team lead us in different games and activities. I'm so thankful for that place, especially living in NYC during these times.

In the gritty years of the 1980s and early 1990s in Manhattan, challenges are just a way of life for many of us, but creativity thrives too. Graffiti murals adorn the cityscape, vibrant expressions everywhere I look. Music pulses through the streets, everything from Madonna to El Gran Combo's infectious rhythms. People yell down the blocks, running to greet each other. There's always noise around, even during the late-night hours. Crime rates are high, and drugs and homelessness lurk on every street corner, even within the confines of our own home.

But within this community on East Sixth Street, I discover something different: shared laughter, adventures, and sisterhood.

One day, the workers at the center gather all of us kids together. "We want you to help us repaint the lobby," they announce, and we practically jump out of our seats in excitement.

I can't believe they want us to be part of this project. As we dip our brushes in paint and carefully cover the walls, I feel valued and included, such a contrast to the feeling of being invisible that I sometimes have at home. I share laughs with my cousins and friends, feeling the sense of belonging I've been longing for.

That evening, I run home to tell mom about our day. "Mami, we painted the whole lobby!" I say, bouncing around in the kitchen. "And they're going to show our work to all the parents!"

She smiles at my excitement. "That's wonderful, mija. I'm so proud of you."

When the day arrives for parents to see our work, I can barely contain myself. All of our names are written on the wooden banister in careful letters. I'm part of something good.

The adults praise us for our work, and we share hugs all around. I'm part of a community. An emotionally supportive community that builds us up instead of tearing us down.

They're like the bullpen our neighborhood needs, ready to step in when families are struggling.

Years later, as a young adult, I find myself drinking too much as a defense mechanism and coping strategy for what I am going through. It is not a proud moment in my life, but it helps me have compassion for Moncho. He had to cope with losing his mother at a tender age in Puerto Rico, a shift in family dynamics, and relocating to New York City at a time when violence and drugs were so easily accessible and the "cool" thing to do in the '70s, '80s, and '90s.

I'm in a relationship where I drink too much. Everyone we hang out with drinks. Most of the events and activities we engage in involve alcohol. I distance myself from friendships that used to be my chosen family. I *think* I'm starting a new life I love.

I get out of the projects.

We both have careers.

We have stable income and little to no debt.

We consistently take care of our responsibilities.

But really, I am living a lie. A lie I tell myself over and over again. "It's just alcohol." "It's not a big deal." I am trying to prove that I am good enough, cool enough. But really, I'm just a young adult with childhood wounds that need healing. And like Moncho, I mistake escapism and avoidance for healing, and I misuse alcohol. It becomes a tool for masking my feelings of vulnerability, shame, and guilt, numbing the pain of trauma and grief.

When we end that relationship, it hurts. Yet, it is one of the best decisions I make for myself in a long time. I reconnect with childhood friends and rebuild meaningful connections that align with my values and morals. I start therapy to work on my childhood trauma and the symptoms of PTSD that trigger depressive and anxious symptoms.

I'd spent many years trying to prove myself to others and being a people pleaser because I thought I wasn't good enough. But through therapy, I begin to understand that I have nothing to prove to anyone. In fact, I'm not for everyone, and that is okay! I am enough!

It's 2014, and my future husband and I are walking home from a dinner date at one of our favorite restaurants in LES. As we stroll down familiar streets, we pass the community center.

To my surprise, it is still there AND it's open.

"Should we go in?" I ask Jose, feeling hesitant. "I don't know who's running it now or if we'd be interrupting something."

Jose takes my hand and pulls me toward the entrance. "Come on, let's just see."

Someone greets us at the door, and I explain how much of a positive impact this center had on my life in the '80s and '90s. "I was one of the kid volunteers from back then," I tell him.

His face lights up, and he walks us directly to the staircase. "You have to see this," he says.

And there it is: the wooden banister covered with names of all the kids from my childhood who helped paint the Sixth Street Community Center. Right in the middle, I find mine:

Jessica Rios

My eyes fill with tears as I trace the letters with my finger.

"It was more than just painting," I whisper remembering Howard Brandstein and Annette Averette (RIP), the founders, who, through their passion for helping our community—specifically on East Sixth Street helped me view NYC and its high crime rate and drug-infested streets through a different lens.

It truly is a concrete jungle that built confidence in me. It helped me believe that I didn't have to succumb to violence or drugs.

They believed in us; they gave me hope for a brighter tomorrow and the courage to refuse to be defined by my circumstances.

The narrative of growing up in NYC with parental substance abuse is a challenging one. Mine has moments of fear, confusion, and a desperate search for stability and to be seen. Yet, within the chaos, there are glimmers of hope, like the safe space provided by the East Sixth Street Center. There I found solace, camaraderie, and a sense of purpose.

As I reflect on my journey, I realize the profound impact of supportive communities in shaping our resilience. I learned to confront my past, seek real healing, and make decisions based on my values and morals.

The legacy of the Sixth Street Center lives on, not just in the memories of painted walls or names on banisters, but in the spirit of its community members, fueled by hope and an unwavering determination to defy the odds. I am reminded that we are not defined by our circumstances but by the strength of our determination to rise above them.

The staff at the East Sixth Street Center were the true relievers of this time in my childhood. They stepped in to help preserve hope for kids like me. Their relief work is measured in the lives they changed, including mine.

ROUNDING THE BASES

Once a ball is hit, it's in play, and the hitter must run their fastest around the bases to reach home without being called "out."

I am eight years old and I want to become a Social Worker. I want to help other people live happier lives. I want them to feel joy. I can't do it by myself, though. Life, like baseball, requires you to round all the bases to reach home. Sometimes you sprint or stumble, but you're always moving forward, toward home. My journey starts when I recognize I want to help others.

Sometimes I overhear adults around me talking about us with worried and sad voices. They talk about all the yelling and fighting they think we see at home. They wonder what we've seen and heard, but sometimes they act like we don't notice anything at all. "Hopefully, they haven't noticed." But no one asks us directly. Maybe they don't want to draw our attention to it, just in case. The truth is they seem worried when they think we see something we shouldn't have. And since I don't want to worry them, I won't mention any of what I see, hear, or understand.

Often though, my stomach is in knots when I hear them talking about us, like a baserunner caught in between bases, unsure which direction to go. The shame burns in my stomach and chest, but I keep my game face on.

Mami uses drugs that change her. They make her calmer and sadder. She cries a lot. The adults around me—my family—blame Moncho for it because he is older than my mom and sold drugs. Others blame her older siblings, friends, and just living in LES during the '70s and '80s. The adults say my dad shouldn't have brought drugs into our home. Maybe they're right. They say, "El es de la calle." But he also loves me and shows me affection and protects his daughters. Moncho, my father, is different from Moncho, my mom's partner, I guess.

When Moncho and mom are drunk or high, they are cool and attentive one moment, and the next, my sis and I are rushing to keep out of the way before they yell at us to go play in our room. They mostly yell at each other, though. Mami and Moncho are affectionate and caring toward us—we feel their love. And even though they're also affectionate with each other, I still see the fear and anger between them. When my dad is using, he gets violent with my mom, and she feels forced to endure it. I'm sure she has her reasons. I don't want that for myself when I'm older in a relationship.

Moncho goes to jail for a drug-related crime. Mami starts a new relationship with a man we call Moré. He supports my mother when she says she wants to stop using drugs, and he wants to help raise us and grow the family. He shows me, my mom, and my sisters love and attention. My family also welcomes Moré by spending birthdays and holidays together. Moré cooks a lot and helps Mom wherever he can, especially when she isn't feeling physically well. He makes these delicious Dominican dishes—one of my favorites is a purple potato salad. He also takes us to my mom's special appointments at a clinic near Delancey Street.

Most people would expect us to be mad at Moré, to think he's trying to replace our dad. But it's the complete opposite. I love Moré and I feel so happy to have a stepfather who cares about Mami and who tells the adults to stop talking about "grown-up stuff" when we're around. Moré is strict but he's funny and fun, too. He rides his bike from Sixth Street to Little Italy where he works at Ferrera baking Italian cakes, but his Dominican cakes taste way better to me. Moré listens to Mom, and he's gentle with her. He doesn't yell at her and he asks how she's feeling. He asks us all how we feel, and my stomach never gets those knots when he's around. With Moré, it feels like we're safe on base instead of always running scared between them.

There are a lot of different people at the clinic. Some come alone and others with children. Some people are smiling, some are upset and hostile, and others are crying, but I'm just curious. My mother, a pillar of strength, always shields herself from vulnerability. She doesn't like to ask for help or show anyone when she's sad. She tells us that if we show our weaknesses or ask for help, people will throw it in our faces later, or we will have to owe them.

But right now, a kind-looking woman approaches us, and miraculously, I see Mami's defenses crumble. I know she takes pride in always being there for us, but in this instance, she's allowing someone to be there for her. Mami shares her story and cries, and I can feel her relief as she takes deep breaths and smiles through the tears. Watching Mami cry with the social worker feels like finally sliding into home plate after an exhausting run around the bases. For the first time, I see what relief looks like on my mother.

I sit with this lady who explains that she and the other workers help individuals and families feel better physically and emotionally. This Social Worker asks us questions in a way that makes me feel safe, seen, and truly understood. We color together as we talk. Well, I mainly talk after she asks questions. In this moment, I know I want to do what she does—I want to step into this important role in someone else's life. I want to have that impact on others like she has with my mom by empowering her and helping her live a healthier life.

When the adults in my family ask what I want to be when I grow up, I tell them, "I want to help people." Some adults laugh, and that makes me feel weird, silly, confused. A family member tells me to focus on school and being a kid. I'm confused about what she means—I am already doing that!

But then, I hear her tell someone else that me and my sister probably won't finish school and will have babies too young because of what's happening with our parents. I feel sad and angry because I know she doesn't believe in me. Also, my parents are good parents! Thankfully, other family members are more encouraging. They tell me how excited they are to see me helping others. One day, my aunt tells my grandmother of my goal, and they talk about how exciting it will be to see me as an adult all dressed up "tan intelligente y bonita ayudando a los pobres." Their praise and encouragement feel good; it gives me hope and confidence.

Mami finishes her treatment at the clinic and is healthier than ever. She rounds her own bases toward recovery. She seems happier, too, except for right now. Right now, she seems nervous and angry. She yells to my sister and me, "Just keep walking!" But why are we walking so fast? *How* is Mami walking so fast with a stroller and two of us holding on to the sides? I turn around quickly. Is that Moncho hiding? Is he following us? He's out here?! Why are we rushing home? Why is Mami mad at him and avoiding him? I'm so confused, but I follow Mom's directives, so she won't get more upset. When we get home, she starts talking to the neighbor. I pretend to play with my sister, but I'm listening. I tell myself my ears have superpowers, but I can't really hear what they are saying.

Later, I get scared that I won't have any parents left. I'm not sure where Moncho is because we don't see him anymore. Maybe he is in jail. Maybe he is in New Jersey where most of his family is. My mother and Moré are doing well. They have one daughter together and another on the way. That's five daughters Mami has. Four sisters for me and I love them so much. When Mami is giving birth to my fourth sister, she has a heart attack. I'm scared. I'm so nervous that she will die and we will lose her, too. I can't lose the only parent left in my life!

My grandma, Mamita/Mami Elsie, tells us that Mom is fine. She is recovering well, and we have nothing to worry about. Phew. That was scary! My sister and I are living with Mamita for a school year while Mom gets our new place ready for all of us in Brownsville, Brooklyn. I'm in the fourth grade. Mom is healthy—she doesn't have to go to the clinic anymore. Mami Elsie explains that Mom will keep getting healthier, so we will spend only one school year with her. And we will go to Mom's on the weekends. I miss being with my mom and my other sisters. My sister and I are told we have to be strong, so I don't cry in front of anyone. Instead, I do it while I'm taking a shower, and when I come out, I tell everyone I keep getting soap in my eyes.

Mamita lives in the Smith Projects, so we live there too until the new place is ready. It's my sister, Mamita, Abuelo, my cousin, my aunt and uncle, and me. I feel so thankful for the Social Worker who helped my mother. Even though we've been uprooted from East Sixth Street, I discover comfort in the structure that my grandmother provides. And it is still in LES—more toward Chinatown and Wall Street area. I'm happy and relieved that, for the first time in a while, change is a rare visitor. Mamita has us on a schedule and I like it. The stability and daily routines feel safe.

Our days are marked by breakfast, school lunches, and set dinners. Mamita wakes up before 6 a.m. On a typical morning, she slowly makes her cup of coffee with her colador (a cloth strainer for coffee). She sits at the end of the table, sipping from her mug and praying on her rosary. Some days, when we wake up and head to the kitchen, she's still praying with her rosaries in hand—she often jokes that her prayers take time because we have a big family to pray for. Other days, she sips her coffee and asks how we slept or if we are looking forward to anything particular in school. She also loves to hear me tell her about my desires to help people when I get older. She tells me how proud she is and reminds me of the importance of education, all while eating delicious ham, egg, and cheese on mayo toast. Sometimes I add ketchup to it. Sometimes I have a cafecito of my own; it *is* a Puerto Rican household after all.

Evenings are dedicated to dinner; homework; laughing with grandparents; and, of course, watching novelas (Spanish soap operas), *Primer Impacto*, and Walter Mercado. I do my homework after eating at the dining room table. Then, I shower and meet Mamita in the living room, where she is on the couch browsing through the latest print of *TeveGuia*—a gossip magazine from Puerto Rico. I sit on the floor with her, waiting for her to pass the *TeveGuia* over while laughing at some ridiculous news stories. Then we gossip about the characters in the novelas. I particularly love *Marimar* and *Dos Mujeres, Un Camino* novelas, which I have no business watching at this age. (This makes them even better!)

The weekends hold their own sacred rituals. Mamita, a devout Catholic, makes sure we don't miss *Sabado Gigante* with Don Francisco while flipping through the latest *TeveGuias*. We also spend the weekends with mom and my sisters in our new home—I'm excited to live there with them soon. On Sundays, Mom makes us commute from Brownsville to the LES to attend mass at St. Brigid's Church with Father George, who has been there for years. He always makes us feel comfortable because he's welcoming and nonjudgmental. My least favorite part is the MTA commute. It takes forever and is boring. One Sunday after mass, we get breakfast at a diner on 8th Street and Avenue A with Mom…and Moncho! I am happy to see him, but I know he comes and goes. Before I know it, it's back to Mamitas to start the school week.

Despite being nicknamed "Prieta Fea" (the ugly dark one, but in an endearing way), my grandmother consistently bestows upon me a sense of beauty. Her praises are a constant melody in my life. We forge an unbreakable bond. I'm sure I can write a whole book inspired by her.

Mamita is confident and brave. She stands up for what is right, and she doesn't care what others think about her. For example, let me tell you about her love-hate relationship with bras. She wears one daily but not all day. One day, we are sitting in a medical waiting room when I see Mamita moving around in her coat. *What is she doing? Ha!* I see her bra in her hand as she slides it through her coat sleeve and into her pocket. She smirks at me, and she knows I see her. I let out a laugh, and she laughs too, hugging me. I feel loved and safe.

My grandfather is a funny character. He enjoys going to the OTB (Off Track Betting) in Chinatown—it's walking distance from home. He bets money on horse races. I don't know if Abuelo works, and I don't even know how he has money for betting. Nonetheless, not my business. That's adult stuff.

I find it super entertaining when Mamita looks at the clock, says the time aloud, and tells us to get dressed. "Vamos pa buscar tu abuelo." Off to the OTB we go with our mischievous smiles. "Abuelo is getting in trouble, AGAIN." My sister and I laugh.

Mamita is a fierce woman, and Abuelo knows that. We laugh at Abuelo because every time we catch him at the OTB, staying later than he should, he turns pale. We tease Abuelo a lot. He doesn't like it because he knows Mamita is really upset at him and it just keeps her anger going, but we find it amusing. We continue to tease him because we know he secretly loves it. Trust me! He always asks if everything is okay when we aren't teasing him. We have a playful relationship, and he enjoys our lighthearted banter. Abuelo is fun and easygoing, and he creates a space where I can be my quirky self. He teaches me not to take life too seriously and encourages me to enjoy being a kid.

I feel safe knowing that I have structure and room to play, a routine that involves love and security.

I miss my mother during the week even though we spend a lot of weekends with her. Missing mom is a constant reminder that living with Mamita is temporary. We will be back home with mom soon enough, but that doesn't take away my sadness from being apart from her and my younger siblings. I don't like being separated from them, and this "short" time feels like an eternity because sadness weighs heavily on me. Even though it's stable here with my grandparents, and I know they love me, I yearn for my parents. I wish they could be the stable ones. Sometimes I even wish they were still together. I know it's not up to me, though.

Each move feels like touching another base: from LES to Mamita's, from Mamita's to Brownsville. Each stop is necessary; each brings me closer to home.

I've been in the Social Work field for over 20 years now. I'm working at my private practice as a Licensed Clinical Social Worker offering services to women and the LGBTQ+ community in New York and Florida, and I have helped empower hundreds of souls!

I'm fortunate to have a home in Florida that I share with my husband and my Frenchie, Mugzy. We moved down to Florida in 2020 during the pandemic. Man, for what we were paying for a one-bedroom in NYC, we were able to invest in a house with a pool! I've always wanted to live in Florida. Moncho did, too, at some point, but he always wanted to stay close to his girls, so he never left NYC. Our home gives me that same sense of security and love I felt with Mamita and Abuelo.

One summer, Mamita and Abuelo come visit me in my new Florida home. AY que bendicion! The first morning after they arrive, I am lying in bed and I can hear whispers and movement coming from my kitchen. It is early, so I leave my room to investigate. Mamita is standing over our kitchen counter in front of the Keurig machine with her cup of coffee, eyes closed as she embraces her Rosario and whispers her prayers. My heart smiles as my mind flashes back to living with Mamita in Smith Projects. There is no longer the colador, but sheer joy and love rushes over me just as it did when I was eight years old.

During a different trip—one I take to NYC—I visit my grandparents. While Mamita is busy in the kitchen, Abuelo and I lie on his bed, joking around and laughing about the silliest things. Mamita walks in with her sassiness and says, "Parecen niños," before walking away. I look over at Abuelo and see he's fallen asleep. In that moment, I feel a deep appreciation for the adults in my life, the ones who encouraged me to pursue an education, who made me feel smart and beautiful, and who accepted my quirky ways. Their support and belief in me have been invaluable. Because of the love and encouragement they gave me and still provide, I've been able to build my life just as I wanted it to be.

Looking back, I see how each base I touched led me toward home plate, which, for me, is a life of helping others make their way around their own bases to truly find their way home.

SAME TEAM, NEW STADIUM

All teams face playing on different fields.

As we approach our new home, my mom, sisters, and Tio, walk beside us. Tio is a loud boisterous Puerto Rican with a no-nonsense attitude who always tells us how important education is and why we should mind our business. I already know these things, but he keeps saying them anyway.

I get it; YA, Tio, I think, but I keep quiet. Though it's annoying to hear the same thing over and over, I'm also very thankful and feel safe and loved because he believes in us rather than feeling sorry for us. Walking from the train station to our three-story building shows me how different this neighborhood is from the towering projects of Manhattan. It's quieter here, less busy than the city. My stomach does flip-flops thinking about our new three-bedroom apartment on the second floor and my new school, PS 284.

The new school year starts and Mom walks us to school, at first. We live on a dead-end street, and all we have to do is walk around the cul-de-sac to get to school. Mom always wants to make sure we're safe, so we don't even get to cross the street.

Ms. Chambers, my fifth-grade teacher, is tall, sweet, and loves the color turquoise. She wears turquoise earrings, rings, necklaces and bracelets. She assigns a project to imagine our future selves. I'm excited but really nervous, too. My hands get sweaty as I stand in front of everyone in class. My heart races, but I smile and tell them my dream of becoming a pediatrician. Ms. Chambers gives me a white lab coat and stethoscope—to make my dream feel more real, I guess. I'm so relieved she doesn't ask me to buy them, because we can't afford things we don't really need. What am I going to do with a lab coat and stethoscope anyway?

Being the new kid in class, I feel the other students being playful but careful around me. Despite my nerves, I am determined to make new friends. Kindness becomes my weapon, slowly breaking down barriers put up by some kids who aren't nice to me at first. I've seen my parents when they're angry; they are still great people underneath the anger, so my classmates must be, too. At lunch, I try double Dutch, but I lack coordination and I'm not very good at it. Since I can't jump well, I learn to turn the rope instead. I tell the others I like turning better than jumping. They are happy with that because they just want to jump, and they're really good. These friendships become like a sisterhood; we share love, values, laughter, and honesty.

We tell each other to do good in school, stick up for ourselves, and just be ourselves. From fifth through eighth grade, everything changes about how I see myself. I start to love the weird things about me, and my friends do, too. I love hip-hop, R&B, Spanish music, pop, and rock. Most kids in Brownsville don't listen to all that. I watch baseball, especially the Yankees, and my classmates think that's weird too, but they don't make fun of me for it. They ask if the Yankees won and laugh when they lose. They're cool with me being different. I figure out how important it is to have friends who like the same things, don't judge you, and have your back. When you're real about who you are, other people want to be real, too. The way they accept me and support me makes me feel like I belong to something bigger.

My friends are like my teammates, and we all learn to play different positions in each other's lives.

My mom, who takes care of five kids by herself, has been through a lot, including losing her father young, moving from

Puerto Rico to NYC, and other hard things that are her story to tell. But she knows how to make things work. She has five kids and doesn't get any child support. We get public assistance with cash and food stamps, and we live in a NYCHA (New York City Housing Authority) apartment with three bedrooms.

I hear what people say about me. They judge me, and that makes me angry. My anger scares me—it's a feeling I'm not comfortable with because anger leads to violence. I see adults around me, including Moncho, get violent when they're angry or have to deal with conflict. So how am *I* supposed to know the right way to be angry? This anger, it's like a fire burning inside me, and I don't know how to let it out without causing harm.

I hear things like: "Oh, you need an education to get out of where you live," but this is my *home* right now. My loving home. Why should I feel rushed out?! They feel sorry for us, and I hate it.

"You're living in that neighborhood with animals." WTF does that even mean?! I have great friends, here my sisters and mother live comfortably, and we're surrounded by love. Sure, there's a lot of crime. I learn quickly that in my community, many people resolve conflict by yelling, fighting, or even shootouts. I'm cautious but not scared. This isn't a zoo. We are not animals! I'm filled with rage when I hear this nonsense from adults. What makes them any better?! Also, they're being racist! I want to yell back, but I can't say anything to them. Instead, I write my feelings and thoughts in a journal or cry in the shower until the rage goes away. We might not be little kids anymore, but we still can't tell adults how we feel, especially not when we're angry at them.

We rely on welfare to make ends meet. Monthly food stamps are our lifeline, turning ordinary purchases into big compras. Not a small comprita. We help Mom down the supermarket's aisles with two large metal carts filled with food, and we head to the register. It is all covered by her monthly food stamp stipend. Our compras don't have the expensive brand cereals, but the generic ones are just as sweet, filled with just as much sugar, if not more. I know some people think food stamps are just handouts and that our NYCHA apartment isn't the best place to live, but I feel grateful. We have food every month and a roof over our heads. That's more than some people have. When I see those carts full of food, I feel happy knowing we won't go hungry. But once that runs out, we must wait for next month's food stamps. We all try not to be wasteful. We only have seconds if we're still *really* hungry. And we love leftovers, too.

But things aren't always good. It isn't all sugary cereals and hostess chocolate cupcakes. I hate hotdogs. Mom boils them too long, so they pop open. Then she wraps them in slices of bread. We have to devour them, or the bread gets super soggy and sticks to our fingers, teeth, and the roofs of our mouths. There is nothing like "broke Puerto Rican food." White rice with a fried egg and ketchup, and rice with spam are my favorites. That's common in our household. Mom has a friend who likes to come over unexpectedly. When she does, she always eats some of our food. Sometimes, Mom rushes us to eat our food before her friend visits because we don't have enough to share. That doesn't feel good, but we can't be without food.

There is talk about the Work & Welfare Reform program in NYC. It's the Giuliani administration, where anyone on public assistance can "Volunteer" to earn a full-time job. I'm intrigued. I hear jokes about cleaning parks or the government trying to make us work for free. That's fucked up and doesn't sound right to me.

I gather up newspaper articles from the *NY Post, NY Daily News, Newsday,* and the *New York Times* that my social studies teacher leaves behind, and I watch the news coverage on different channels to get different perspectives and learn as much as I can. It seems like a great opportunity, especially for a single mom with no higher education degree or much work experience.

Mom goes to an appointment and returns to tell us she

signed up for the program. She doesn't seem too enthusiastic, but I am. After some time, Mom secures a full-time position as a custodian in a college in downtown Brooklyn. She'll have a salary with full city benefits, like retirement and good health insurance. This is amazing! A career for my mother. I'm proud of her! We all are!

She comes home exhausted. And we tell her how proud we are of her. She can practice English now, too. She understands and speaks it a little, but she needs to practice more to be confident in what she's saying. She has a sense of purpose in life. It's more than just us to get up for. She can rely on herself instead of men. She's more confident. It's admirable. And she is making meaningful connections.

Mom's budgeting skills ensure we can go on school trips, savoring hot hero sandwiches, fifty-cent sodas, and chips from 3 M's deli on Mother Gaston. Sometimes, I indulge in a Chick-O-Stick. Okay, a lot of Chick-O-Sticks. We make it work, and every bit of it is appreciated; though, in private, I write in my journal how grateful I am *and* how nice it would be to have a little more money for extra food, snacks, and clothes. It is my aspiration to pursue a higher level of education and a career that promises a substantial salary. I want a salary that can afford any cereals, meals from any restaurant, and whatever my family and friends desire at any given moment. Many of my friends' houses are just a few blocks away. One of their mothers works for the city and can afford everything I dream of. I don't know what she does, but I know she works for the city, and it comes with a salary and private health insurance. The end goal is to have city benefits. I have another friend whose mother works within the community and could afford more brand clothes for my friend. I feel jealous because I get teased for my clothes not being name-brand or being bootleg/fake. I keep that feeling of shame inside of me and in my journals.

I take care of my clothes, though! I hang my one FILA sweater, two FILA sweats (real, *not* bootleg), regular sweaters, baggy shirts, tights, and jeans. We go shopping at Conway and

Rainbow often. On school days, I wear a uniform even though they're not required, a reminder of our financial struggles because we can't all afford a whole wardrobe. I tell myself that school isn't about clothes as I get teased for what I'm wearing. It's a time for learning, forging friendships, and questioning teachers about the world beyond Brownsville. That is all I keep in mind, and I stay focused on what I can control. I am instilled with a profound sense of purpose and determination!

Things aren't perfect in Brownsville, but I have my friends and my family, and I hope that things will get better. Even if I'm playing in a different stadium now, I'm learning the rules of the game, and sometimes changing stadiums isn't so bad after all.

CURVE BALLS

**Curved pitches that make it harder
for a batter to hit the ball.**

Things keep changing in my life, like curveballs you never see coming.

In the heart of Brooklyn, my sister, Mimi, and I sit on the kitchen counter gazing out the window. Our outings are limited, especially when the streets bear witness to more violence than we want to think about. Only when the snow blankets the ground are we allowed to venture out, the world temporarily hushed by the falling snowflakes. Mami knows not many like the cold weather, so we are in less danger. She watches us from the window when we are allowed out.

But the window holds more than just a view. It cradles memories, like my sister perched on the windowsill, waiting for our father's arrival. Her backpack ready, waiting for adventures with him, her joyful cry of "Dad is here!" making us all excited. My stomach always turns watching my sister at the window, her fingers pressed against the glass like a fan waiting at the stands for an autograph that might never come. I feel the weight of her hope like a heavy bat on my shoulders, and I want to protect her from the strikeout I know is coming, from being disappointed again.

Moncho is a man of light and laughter who knows a little about everything. I love sitting in his pickup truck, stuck in traffic on the way to Jersey, as he tells tales of construction, the city's history, and his childhood in Morovis, Puerto Rico. But it is his talk of baseball that catches my fascination and attention, his words leaving me hungry for more.

Then there are the hours Mimi spends in hope, eyes fixed

out the window. Her pain is palpable, and it pains me to witness it. I try every diversion, from play to pestering, but nothing stops her longing. Her connection with our father is unique and special, a bond I come to cherish and understand. I never ask her how she feels about him not showing up, how it feels to be stood up. I see the hope in her eyes, a yearning for his return, a wish for an unending stream of his love.

I learn not to tether my heart too tightly. People, especially men, seem to drift in and out whenever they want. Our waiting doesn't matter to them; they don't care about the ache that comes with it—the wait for change, for sobriety, for something more. And then, Moncho returns, a surprise in itself. But his presence is always short lived. He comes, and then he is gone.

I learn also to watch for signs that things are going wrong again, like a batter trying to guess what pitch is coming next. I don't want to have to be good at this, but I am.

Our landline is ringing. Mom shuts the door as if we can't hear her yell, "¡Puñeta, otra vez!" My dad isn't showing up. No surprise to me. My mom tries her best to keep us busy at home. We don't do any recreational activities, so we listen to music, watch what we can on TV, use our imagination, read, and even watch our stepfather, Moré, in the kitchen. Moré loves to cook and bake his butt off in the kitchen. His cooking is why I love Dominican food, particularly cakes. Give me a Dominican cake or a Valencia cake and I am GOOD! He is here when he isn't working, especially during times like these, when we're disappointed my father doesn't come. He never talks negatively about Moncho, at least not to us. Moré is consistent.

Until he and mom call it quits.

I feel a deep sadness for my two youngest sisters because of the changes they are going through. This is a really hard time for them, I assume. Moré, their dad, is a strict but loving person. He teaches us the importance of leading with love and standing up for ourselves. When he and Mom separate and he moves to The Heights, we stay connected, visiting him often. He, Mom, and Moncho manage to keep a good relationship.

Everything feels strange at home when Moncho moves in with us in Brooklyn. It isn't just a change in who lives here but a change that stirs up so many emotions in me.

And things aren't so smooth with everyone *else*, either. Right before Moncho moves in, Mimi decides to move out to live with her boyfriend, which adds another layer of complexity to our family dynamic. She and Mom fight constantly. My sister just wants more of our dad around and for my mom to listen to her. I feel so much compassion and sadness for her. We cope with our father's absence differently. I have moments of missing him, but I understand and accept that I can't force him to be present. In fact, I don't want to. I focus on the things that I can control.

Her decision to move in with her boyfriend makes me incredibly nervous. They aren't adults yet, and I don't trust him. He seems controlling, but she moves in with him and his mom anyway. I can't understand her logic and hate seeing her and Mom at odds. They butt heads so much because of how similar they are. Even with all their similarities, they don't understand each other. They were both separated from their dads at a young age and felt not heard by their parents, especially their mothers.

But in the midst of all this, I *am* excited about finally having my own room. I think it's something I deserve for being the rule follower, attending school, and not giving my mother a hard time. No more sharing—it is a small silver lining.

Mom tells Moncho that Mimi ran away and moved in with her boyfriend. Mom asks him to convince her to come back home. To our surprise, my sister refuses, and Moncho moves in with us instead.

I am confused, happy, cautious, and fearful all at once. Why would Moncho and Mami want to live together when they don't get along? Why are they making this decision? I am afraid that Moncho will get violent with Mom again, so I warn him that if he ever lays a finger on her, I will call the police. I mean it! Also, I tell him there are no drugs allowed in our home. He assures me he isn't using and wouldn't harm her. He looks healthy, and I want to believe him, but I know addiction is difficult to manage.

Despite my doubts, I am still happy about what is happening. I'm happy that he moves in. I'm happy to have Moncho around. I love being in his presence when he is sober. But I can't help but wonder: How will he maintain sobriety while working full time in construction and living with four girls and my mom? Five females with five different personalities—it is chaotic at times, and I fear it will be too chaotic for his sobriety. I never lose faith in Mom's sobriety, though. She's resilient!

To my surprise, Moncho steps in and takes my sisters in as his own, referring to them as his daughters, even with our friends. We watch baseball games together, and he helps Mom financially. I know he is trying to win my trust, and I take advantage of that, asking for the latest Jordans and Nikes, mostly uptowns. He is happy that I'm doing well in school, so he buys them for me when he can. Mom, too. She gets me my first red and white Jordan 12's on Pinkin Avenue.

My room becomes my sanctuary, filled with posters of the Yankees, Derek Jeter, Jennifer Lopez, Ricky Martin, Marc Anthony, Biggie, JayZ, *NSYNC, 98 Degrees, Britney Spears—the works. I even have my own landline phone. It is clear with a long, curly cord. It's fun chatting with friends or playing pranks when we aren't in school. That *67 option is entertaining. I feel confident, worthy, and secure.

But everything changes when I'm in the eleventh grade. Mimi is in a domestic violence situation, and our dad is livid. I'm livid, too, because I know this will cause *more* change in our lives, and things are *finally* going well for me. Moncho picks up my sister from her boyfriend's house—she has a bruised eye. Seeing her walk in with her head down in shame breaks my heart. I hope she'll learn from this situation and not return to him. She is back home. But "home" quickly becomes a battleground.

A few days later, Moncho hears my sister's boyfriend outside our door and tells us to stay inside with the door locked. We don't listen. Peeking through the peephole, we watch as my dad confronts him. I can't make out what he says, but suddenly, they are fighting, tumbling down a flight of stairs. We rush out to ensure Moncho doesn't get hurt, and in the chaos, I am filled with fear and rage—anger at the dirtbag for hitting my sister, at my parents for not meeting her needs, at my sister for being in a relationship with that douchebag, and then at my sister's boyfriend again for being abusive to my sister and other females as well.

After the fight, we are forced to call the cops. They advise us to get an emergency safety transfer as they don't think we will ever be safe in our home again. We stay with my grandmother briefly while figuring out the logistics. Moncho's shoulder is injured, and he needs medical attention. My heart aches for Fluffy, my pet rabbit, but Mom keeps insisting it is too dangerous to go back and get him. How is he going to survive?

Ultimately, it is decided that Mom, my sisters, and I will enter the shelter system as the only way to get the emergency transfer. Moncho can't join us because NYCHA doesn't know he was living with us. Shortly after we move, he relapses, which only further fuels my anger. Anger that I do not dare release because I think it will cause more stress on the others. I am tired of everyone making stupid and selfish decisions! Sadness doesn't seem to creep in until I'm alone, but mostly, it is anger at the lack of common sense and better judgment in the adults around me. *Here we are, displaced yet again.* I'm just a teenager just trying to hold it together.

The only way I can cope is by clinging to what I know, which is school and volunteering. I don't miss a day of class and keep up with my volunteer duties at the Department for the Aging. I find solace in talking with the senior citizen I'm paired with, discussing everything from living your dreams to death and dying. I'm fascinated by death. I view it as a transition and see it as the only guarantee in life. Also, I have amazing friends who shower me with love and support.

But then, *change*, yet again. Even though my mom told me not to, my best friend, Ely, and I return to Brownsville to check on Fluffy, and we find him dead in his cage. I can't contain my tears. Fluffy's death crushes me. I knew that he wouldn't live forever, but I feel so sad and guilty. I didn't feed him. I *couldn't* feed him. From this moment, I vow that I will create a stable future, free from crisis and drama—one where Fluffy could thrive. I refuse to live in fear of violence the way my mother and sister have.

For about seven weeks, we bounce from shelter to shelter in the Bronx, lugging our bags around, hoping our emergency transfer will come through soon. Not everyone deals with it as well as I do, and it breaks my heart to see my family struggle. I help my mother navigate the psychiatric system, help my little sisters with homework assignments, and try to keep a positive attitude. I still cry only in the shower, where no one can see or hear me. I am exhausted and frustrated, but I have to stay strong, ever the rule follower, the strong one, the one everyone else relies on.

Each new shelter feels like another new game, playing on unfamiliar fields and with different rules. My grief for Fluffy, my anger at the adults, and my fear for my sisters all sit heavy in my chest. But I can't let myself strike out. I have to keep on swinging.

Finally, there is good news: our emergency transfer is approved! We move to a NYCHA apartment in the South Bronx. I don't care about the old rivalry between Brooklyn and the Bronx. If you are from either borough, you never travel to the other borough unless you have to. But I just want a safe home. So, I adapt. We all do. Plus, I am walking distance from Yankee stadium now! I attend games and sit in the bleachers for just $8. Ely and I sit with the Bleacher Creatures (season ticket holders made up of fun and rowdy mostly grown men) and have a ball, cheering and booing the other teams.

My senior year of high school is a whirlwind of emotions. I spend time with friends, watch the Yankees, and wait for my college acceptance letters while navigating yet another change at home. Moncho is living with us again in the Bronx. I find my father's behavior suspicious, and I assume he is using again. He wants to meet with us and I just *know* he is going to let us know about his recent drug use. But he announces he is moving out to live in Manhattan instead, and I am strangely relieved. I hug him and ask him how I can help. I feel a deep sense of joy knowing that I can have a better relationship with each parent now that they are physically separated again. I never thought my parents were meant to be together forever, and now this chapter is finally closing.

When I receive my acceptance letter from Lehman College, I am over the moon. Ely gets into her SUNY school, and two of my other best friends, Marsha and Noelia, are also accepted to Lehman. We are going to college! It is the light at the end of a very dark tunnel.

Graduation is a celebration of survival and success. My friends and I take pictures, laugh, and reflect on the challenges and memories of the past four years. Moncho is there, as always, supporting me in my big moments. My parents are finally getting along, but thankfully, they aren't together. I hope my sisters follow their dreams and stay in school, just as I have.

Walking across the stage at graduation, I feel proud. My friends, family, and teachers have helped me through all the hard times. Now I'm ready for college, ready to keep moving forward. I know how to handle the curveballs life throws at me now. I just keep my eye on the ball and swing.

DIGGING IN

Before a pitch is thrown, the hitter readies himself by digging his cleats into the dirt to gain firm footing.

On September 11, 2001, I'm in class when the class clown mentions the city is under attack. We are annoyed at him for joking about that. He often jokes around, interrupting the class with his nonsense. Little do we know, he is telling the truth—his aunt had called his cell phone to let him know. Our professor looks puzzled. He asks everyone to stay calm until he can figure out what is happening. Then, he confirms it: two planes flew into the World Trade Center. We are sent home. I feel such immense fear because I am not sure what is happening. My grandparents live not too far from the World Trade Center. Are they okay? My sister is going to school also not too far. Is she okay?

I think of the many memories we made at the World Trade Center. We would go for Hispanic night and other festivities. I remember meeting one of the members of the Barrio Boyzz and a few other salseros as well. We'd walk from my grandmother's home to the WTC. Those are great memories, but this attack is not one of them. I feel fear like I never thought I could feel before. And my childhood best friend, Tice - she was so far from home. We are in the northern part of the Bronx. I live in South Bronx and she lives in Brownsville. We are walking on the Concourse and people are yelling, frantic, not knowing if their family members are safe. Of course, she stays with me until her aunt can pick her up, but seeing the fear in her eyes devastates me. There is nothing more I can do. I am so thankful that she is able to be with her family. At home, we are glued to the television, watching the horror of the attacks.

Now, as the fear starts to fade, I feel helpless and guilty. I wish I was already a social worker who could help those in need, but I am only a freshman in college. There is nothing I can do. All the things my family and I have gone through that previously felt unfair seem minute compared to all this. I feel this deep sense of guilt for being safe. Manhattan is often a target, but no one cares about the South Bronx. That is a good thing, right?! But I still feel guilty. This event changes me forever. It changes so many people! I know there is more I can do if I continue my studies and earn my social work degree to help my community and my city—New York City!

I turn to baseball, which returns a week after the attacks. That week with no baseball felt like an eternity to me. I study for hours with the news in the background, and I hear these horrible stories of family members searching for their loved ones and not being able to find them in the rubble or having to learn of their passing. They say baseball is America's pastime, and that's never more true than during this postseason. It is a much-needed distraction. Bringing baseball back makes me feel like we're showing the world that we aren't afraid and won't let anyone stop us from living our lives.

The Yankees are back in the Bronx, and President Bush throws out the first pitch of Game 3. We have fallen behind 0–2 to the Diamondbacks. We feel united and hopeful and comforted and inspired in such a dark time in NYC and America.

Baseball brings us back to normalcy. Baseball gives us a reason to feel okay again. Even though I still feel guilty about being happy when so many people are suffering, watching the game helps me forget for a little while. Baseball gives me a *reason* to feel okay, an acceptable reason to feel joy again. And maybe even peace. Growing up with constant change, watching baseball has always been one of the things that brings me peace. In those three hours, we lose ourselves for nine innings (sometimes more), and the game holds our grief while giving us permission to hope again.

When we gather in our living rooms, taverns, or bodegas, baseball gives us a safe space to process our emotions. It isn't about forgetting. How could we ever forget what has happened? No, it is about finding healthy ways to remember and cope together.

We are excited about winning a World Championship. Derek Jeter is named Mr. November after hitting a game-winning home run. As a New Yorker, I feel that we *have* to win. The Yankees are going to pull through! We got this! We - as if I am the one behind that plate.

But we lose! It is crushing. We are disappointed, but I also feel so proud of this team and our country for sticking together to get as far as we do.

I am proud to see the stories of others helping in any way they can, whether it is on Ground Zero or in hospitals and mental health clinics. I am grateful that they are able to play these games in the Bronx, in New York City. Grateful for good humans! They give us hope for the next season. I look forward to spring training in 2002.

Even though we lost the World Series, I know we'll get through this together. We're New Yorkers, and we keep moving forward no matter what.

THE CLUBHOUSE

**The players' locker room, a safe sanctuary
where players can be themselves.**

The familiar rumble of Moncho's little red car fills the morning air as we drive through the Bronx. This car is not in good shape, but he loves it. The Puerto Rican flag and rosary sway gently from the rearview mirror. I'm grateful to skip the train commute today, but more than that, I'm grateful for this moment with my father. Moncho exudes this new energy. He is optimistic, motivated, and determined. He is also a bit nostalgic.

"Remember when Derek Jeter got all that criticism about his defense back in '05?" Moncho asks, keeping his eyes on the road. "But he went and won another Gold Glove anyway."

I smile, knowing where he's going with this. "Yeah, like you always say, Moncho—people will doubt you, but you have to set your own standards." I learned early on that your performance on and off the "field" will speak for itself, when playing sports, in your career, battling health conditions, or whatever is going on in your life.

"Exactly, daughter. Like you did at Lehman College that same year." He glances at me proudly.

"Those were some long nights," I say, laughing. "But worth it. I remember when my stepdad would help me fight to stay awake studying those late nights." I have always been an early sleeper. My stepdad's presence was a reminder of love, support, and stability. Graduating from college was a significant milestone, but the true accomplishment was in celebrating with my family, especially Moncho.

"I was so happy when you came to my graduation." Moncho's hands tighten slightly on the steering wheel.

"I know I wasn't always...at my best during those years. People would say things..."

Growing up, I knew people judged Moncho for his substance abuse. I'd hear them say things like, "When is he going to get it together for these girls?" But it isn't that easy! It takes me some time to understand, but I learn that substance abuse is like having a medical condition that needs treatment. As I start to better understand that sobriety is a process; I also learn that grief is not always tied to death. Grief manifests in other forms, like watching a loved one battle addiction. It is hard seeing my dad healthy for a few months and then seeing him wither away again. When Moncho is sober, I ask him questions about his life. For the most part, there is sadness. Sadness around losing his mother at such a young age, relocating from Puerto Rico to New Jersey and New York, and other internal battles.

"Moncho, stop. I know that addiction is like any other medical condition. It needs treatment, patience..."

"And understanding," he adds softly. "You give me that, even when I don't deserve it."

One thing is for sure, Moncho loves his children and grandchildren. In every conversation, he always mentions how much he loves us: his girls, son, and grandchildren. He tells me we are his motivation, and he has hope that one day he will overcome his substance abuse. I've spent most of my life pushing Moncho away to protect myself. I didn't want him to think I would enable him. I don't think these behaviors are okay. But mostly, it just makes me sad to see Moncho fade away when he is using. I never want to see him that way, so I think the best thing I can do for myself is to avoid him until he is clean again. It is a rollercoaster of emotions: sad, angry, worried, relieved, repeat.

Now that I have accepted Moncho's journey to sobriety, I can start to heal. I respect Moncho's journey. I start to feel my father's love again. His love looks like having deep conversations, even if they are while we are watching the Yankees play; feeling his hugs; being silly and laughing; and so much more. Healing, like sobriety, requires patience and time. There's a quote from Clarence Budington Kelland that has always resonated with me: "My father didn't tell me how to live; he lived and let me watch him do it."

"You always deserve it, Moncho."

I often wonder if I can do more for my father. Am I enough? Although I understand his substance abuse isn't my fault, those doubts still creep in. However, what I've learned from him is that kindness, transparency, trust, respect, and love go a long way in maintaining meaningful connections, even when things don't go as planned. Moncho extends those values to me, which deepens our bond despite his struggles.

"Remember 2008? Taking EJ to see A-Rod's home run? You holding him on your shoulders with that bag of Cracker Jacks?" I ask. Alex Rodriguez hit his 35th home run and 100th RBIs (runs batted in) in 12 seasons. Just one more than Babe Ruth.

"You also attended that All-Star game at the stadium," he reminds me.

"Moncho, I asked you to come with me, but you said you had to work!" He asked me so many questions about that game. I was of course happy to share my experience with him and also sad, because I wished he was there with me. After a trip to Florida, before the All-Star game, Moncho returned sober. I was so proud of him and wanted to spend every moment I could with him.

He chuckles. "And that Christmas when you tried to fool everyone with the restaurant food!"

"Hey! My plating was perfect!" I protest, laughing. "Until you went detective mode and found those aluminum trays."

I hosted Christmas for my family for the first time in 2008. Moncho quickly realized I had fibbed about cooking. Growing up, my grandma and mom told me I didn't have to worry about cooking as long as I continued to attend school and establish a career. I took that to heart! I hated cooking! I like it more now because it brings people together, but don't ask me to cook a big meal for a crowd. Well, for that Christmas gathering, I placed an order from one of my favorite Puerto Rican restaurants in el barrio with dinner and dessert. Oh, my plating was on point! *They'll never know*, I thought. But while we were playing games in the living room, dressed in our cute pajamas, I heard something going on in the kitchen. My father busted me! He kept asking if I had really cooked and, of course, I said yes. His suspicion grew so strong he went into the garbage to find all of the aluminum trays the food came in. It was hilarious! We all laughed and carried on. The next day, my older sister told me that it made him so happy to be part of our gathering because he felt included, and he knew I was proud of him.

That holiday gathering was transformed into our family clubhouse where Moncho could just be Dad and where laughter replaced burdens of past struggles.

"A father knows," he says, winking. "Just like I knew you'd make it to Fordham. Speaking of which..." He stops at a red light, turning to face me. "I'm going to be there for your graduation. Sober. That's a promise."

Now, I am in an accelerated master's program at Fordham University, on track to graduate in May of 2009. I remember, he was there at my eighth grade, high school, and undergraduate graduations.

I feel tears welling up. "I know you will be, Moncho. You're different now. I can see it."

"Like the Yankees in spring training this year, new stadium, new energy. I can feel that championship coming." Moncho replies.

"Everything changes, doesn't it?" I say softly. "The old stadium, new beginnings..."

"Change is guaranteed, daughter. But so is love. That never changes." He reaches over and squeezes my hand. "My love for you, your sisters, your brother, the grandkids. That's constant. Like baseball. The players change, the stadium changes, but the game stays the same."

"And you'll always be my MVP, Moncho," I say, squeezing his hand back and then ruining the moment with a different truth…"We are so corny."

The city traffic moves around us, but in this little red car, time seems to stand still. Every memory, every struggle, every triumph—they're all here with us, like baseball cards in a treasured collection. And like Jeter proving his critics wrong, like the Yankees' pursuit of championships, we keep moving forward, one day at a time, one game at a time.

The rosary swings gently as we turn a corner. In this moment, in his little red car, everything feels possible.

THE CONTRACT

An official document that binds a player and a team.

Why did you want this tattoo?" asks the tattoo artist. Why did I choose to permanently etch the iconic Yankee logo into my skin? As I sit in that tattoo parlor, I realize it is about far more than just baseball. It is about honoring memories, processing grief, and marking a turning point in my life. It is a binding agreement with myself. A permanent commitment to honor not just the Yankees, but my own path forward.

On July 13, 2010, George Steinbrenner, the larger-than-life owner of the New York Yankees, passed away. As a lifelong Yankee fan, his death strikes me deeply. Steinbrenner is a controversial figure, no doubt. Some players loved him, others not so much. But that isn't the point. To me, he embodies passion, drive, and an unwavering commitment to his team. His relentless pursuit of victory is something I can't help but admire.

When Steinbrenner died, I text a few friends, fellow Yankee fans, and we mourn together. Just two days later, we are hit with more heartbreaking news: Bob Shepherd, the legendary public address announcer for the Yankees, has also passed away at ninety-nine. Even knowing his age doesn't make it easier to process. Steinbrenner and Shepherd represent something more than simply their roles with the team. They are part of the Yankees' soul, and their loss leaves a void that feels impossible to fill.

So yes, I walked into this tattoo shop inspired to honor Steinbrenner and Shepherd. But the truth behind my desire for this tattoo runs even deeper.

As the artist preps my skin, we begin talking about baseball, and I find myself reflecting on how much the sport has shaped me. Baseball isn't just a game. It is a bridge that connects me to people I love, especially Moncho. From the Yankees dynasty of the late '90s to the 2009 World Series, I have beautiful memories with friends and family, celebrating victories and sharing the joy of the game.

I vividly remember going to games with other Yankee fans like Ely. We are inseparable during those years, sharing in the highs and lows of every season. I recall the 2010 Yankees home opener when Derek Jeter and Joe Girardi present Steinbrenner with his 2009 World Series championship ring. That is the last time I see Steinbrenner in the stadium.

This isn't my first baseball-related tattoo. My first is a rusty baseball with a halo, on my wrist, for Moncho. We never failed to connect through baseball, and that tattoo grows dearer to my heart every day. Now, I want something to commemorate a new chapter, something meaningful that celebrates the impact of Steinbrenner and Shepherd on my life, so I choose the Yankee logo.

As I share some of my favorite baseball memories with the tattoo artist—my first Yankees game; first post season game; Moncho stealing dirt from the house that Ruth built during its last season; EJ, my nephew, rooting for every player who was at bat; celebrating victories at Yankee Tavern; getting food at McDonald's with Ely prior to the game; sitting in my favorite section, the bleachers—I get tearful. Grief has changed me. The loss of Steinbrenner and Shepherd mirrors deeper personal grief I carry: the loss of my father, unresolved pain from my past, and the feeling of being stuck in a life I am not happy with. Right now, I am struggling with low self-esteem, drinking too much, and staying in an unhealthy relationship. I am not proud of who I am, and it is hard to see a way out.

The tattoo artist, like many tattoo artists, becomes a therapist for the day. We talk about what I miss most: healthy relationships, feeling comfortable in my own skin, being surrounded by people who accept and love me unconditionally. As I open up, I find myself diving into memories and struggles I have been avoiding.

Growing up, I am always skinny. At one point, I am even nicknamed "Bones." At the time, I love and embrace it. It is part of who I am, as natural to me as my love for baseball. But somewhere along the way, things change. I start to compare myself to others, and I am plagued by thoughts like, *Am I too skinny? My boobs and butt are too small. I could probably have a smaller waistline.*

To cope with these insecurities and the growing pains of life, I turn to alcohol. I consume way too much, surrounded by a culture that normalizes excessive drinking. Waking up with hangovers and experiencing blackouts are frighteningly common occurrences. Like I am trying to blur out the person I am becoming, the person I don't want to see in the mirror.

And now, I find myself in a relationship, continuing to make choices I am not proud of. I am so far removed from the confident, baseball-loving "Bones" of my youth that I don't even recognize myself anymore. It is like I have lost my home game advantage, playing on a field where the grass feels different under my cleats, and I don't know the rules or even recognize my teammates.

My voice cracks as I share these painful truths with the tattoo artist, as I describe waking up not remembering how I got home. I admit that I look in the mirror and don't recognize the person staring back at me. The steady buzz of the tattoo gun becomes a soundtrack to my confession, and somehow the physical pain of the needle makes it easier to voice the emotional pain I've been carrying.

"You know what's crazy?" I say, watching him carefully outline the N and Y. "I used to be so sure of myself. I knew exactly who I was - this skinny kid who could tell you Derek Jeter's batting average from seasons ago, who would drag anyone to a Yankees game just to share that feeling of being part of something bigger."

He pauses for a moment, wipes away excess ink, and looks up at me. "What happened to her?"

The question hangs in the air between us. I feel tears building up as I realize I have neglected the core of who I am, losing my sense of self in the process. When did I stop being "Bones"? The girl who wore her nickname like a badge of honor, who found joy in keeping score with a pencil and paper, who believed she deserved love without conditions.

"I think I got scared," I mumble. "Scared that being myself wasn't enough. So, I started changing my body, my habits, my relationships. I thought if I could just be different, better, more…I don't know, more *something*, then maybe I'd be worthy of the love I was craving."

The tattoo artist nods while the needle moves steadily across my skin. Each puncture reminds me that I'm choosing to mark this moment permanently. He asks, "And how's that working out for you?"

His question, direct but gentle, makes me laugh. "Not so well. I'm in a marriage that makes me feel smaller every day. I drink to numb feelings I'm afraid to face. I wake up hungover and ashamed, promising myself I'll do better, and then I do it all again the next weekend."

As he fills in the navy blue of the Yankees logo, I watch the familiar symbol take shape on my forearm. The Yankees logo I am about to have etched on my skin really isn't just about baseball anymore. It is about reclaiming that part of me that has gotten lost. The part that is confident, that loves fiercely, that finds joy in the simplicity of each play in a game.

"You know what Steinbrenner would do if he had a player who wasn't performing?" I ask, more to myself than to him.

"Cut them," he answers, without looking up.

"Exactly. He wouldn't keep a player out of pity or because he felt bad about letting them go. He'd make the tough decision for the good of the team. Maybe it's time I started thinking of myself as the general manager of my own life." I feel the weight of my own words.

The tattoo artist smiles, and it seems like he understands what I'm really saying. This isn't just about getting a tattoo to honor two men who died. This is about honoring the woman I used to be and the woman I still have the potential to become.

"That girl, Bones, she is still in there," he says. "She's just been playing on the bench for too long. Maybe it's time to put her back in the game."

As the final details of the logo come together, I feel something shifting inside of me. Each drop of ink being permanently embedded into my skin feels like a promise and not just to remember Steinbrenner and Shepherd, but to remember myself. To remember that I deserve better than settling for a life that makes me feel like a stranger in my own body.

While I'm checking out the final result, the tattoo artist asks, "Why don't you just leave? You're smart, young, beautiful. Why stay in something that doesn't make you happy?"

My automatic response is, "I'm committed to my marriage."

His reply is a revelation: *"Commit to yourself."*

Soon after my tattoo therapy session, I take a trip to Florida with Marsha, and I visit my beloved aunt, grandfather, uncle, and cousins. I reconnect with an old high school friend and have a blast. On this trip, I realize I want more from life, but I am still not ready to make the huge decision to leave my marriage.

But thirteen years later, the tattoo artist's words echo in my heart: *Commit to yourself…*

One night, the police are called after a big altercation with my partner. As much as I am not proud of the behaviors that lead to this, I am grateful for this moment. It is my turning point.

I am done! I finally decide to choose myself, to commit to myself, and to worry only about my *own* contract with *life.*

Getting that Yankee logo tattoo was more than just an act of remembrance for Steinbrenner and Shepherd. It was a seed for the moment I decided to commit to myself, to reclaim my voice, and to make the changes I needed to live the life I want. Grief has transformed me. But like a baseball team after a tough season, I know I have the strength to rebuild and find joy again.

When I look at the Yankee logo on my skin, I remember the lessons I've learned from the game and the people who loved it. It's a symbol of resilience, of the ability to face loss and come back stronger. Most importantly, it's a permanent mark of the day I opened up to the idea of choosing to step up to the plate and take a swing at a better life.

In baseball, as in life, there are no guarantees. But every time I look at my tattoo, I am reminded of my rich experiences and the joy of hanging out as a Bleacher Creature, the love shared with family and friends over countless games, the pain of loss, and the courage to change. And that, more than anything, is why I wanted that Yankee logo tattooed on my body. It's not just a team logo; it's the story of how I find my way back to myself. It is about honoring myself: the skinny kid nicknamed "Bones" who loves baseball, the young adult who lost her way, and the woman I am becoming who is ready to face her demons and step back up to the plate.

OLD TIMERS' DAY

A game day honoring retired players.

I believe in cultivating meaningful connections and relationships. Not the superficial kind. Small talk makes me awkward unless I genuinely don't like someone, which is rare. This dedication to deep connections has shaped my life, especially in how I've experienced loss and found unexpected father figures along the way.

When I lost Moncho, it came after a precious year of his sobriety, when I finally felt like a daddy's girl again. I know what having a Girl Dad feels like. Those visits where he would cook for us, our deep conversations about life and politics flowing as naturally as the food from his kitchen. He would pull me in for these embraces that made me feel so small despite my height—Moncho was taller than me, and I'm tall. In those hugs, I felt both protected and powerful.

The last time I saw Moncho with clear eyes, truly present in his sobriety, was at my niece Dalia's birthday party at a McDonald's in the South Bronx. Kids were loving the slides and ball pits. My nephew had been cranky all day, not feeling well, and he'd found his way into Moncho's arms.

I listened from across the room as Moncho talked to someone nearby, my nephew curled against his chest. "What I didn't do for my girls and son," he said, his voice carrying that heavy weight of confession, "I'm making up for with my grandkids."

The pride in his voice was unmistakable. But it broke my heart.

I couldn't let him carry that guilt, especially on a day meant for celebration. I rushed over and wrapped my arms around both him and my nephew. "Be quiet," I told him, pressing close. "Don't say that. I never wanted you to feel guilty about those years."

He looked at me with those clear eyes I'd been afraid I'd never see again and pulled me tighter into the embrace. In that moment, I was so proud of who he had become. He wore his oversized gray sweatsuit, soft, and smelling like cologne and these caramel treats he used to eat, his signature scent. His arms were strong around me, protective, making me feel small despite my height.

When it was time to leave, we walked to the parking lot together. The McDonald's PlayPlace behind us felt like the end of something, though I didn't know what yet.

"I love you," he said, pulling me in for one more hug. Then he asked, "Who loves you?" He usually played this little game, and when he asked this question, we'd have to answer, "You love us!"

Sometimes I'd tease him, answering "Jesus! Jesus loves me!" instead, just to watch him roll his eyes before we'd all laugh.

"I love you too, Moncho," I said, not knowing these would be our last words to each other, not knowing this would be our last goodbye, with him clear-eyed and present.

Days later, as he lay in the hospital bed, I rubbed his legs and feet, asking one last time, "Who loves you, Moncho?" Through my tears, I answered my own question: "Jesus…and me. Me and Jesus."

His passing created a void in my heart, reopening wounds from the years when drugs had taken him from us emotionally. Yet, I found myself blessed with other father figures who stepped into my life...

On Super Bowl Sunday in 2013, Serrano, a beloved friend from the New York Armory's 69th Regiment Infantry called me up. He was more than a friend; he was an uncle, a father, a brother all rolled into one. We met through Mimi, when they worked together at the Armory.

"Mira. What are you wearing?" asked Serrano.

"Yankees sweats and a Giants T-shirt," I replied.

"Great. Come downstairs now." I looked out the window, and sure enough, he was there. His greeting was, "We are going to the armory to watch the Super Bowl." And even though I was settled on the couch with my cat, ready to watch the game, I was not going to tell him no.

This was the man who helped refinish my apartment floors, accepting only beer as payment, working to salsa music with pride and joy. But that simple description doesn't capture the full spirit of Serrano, who helped anyone he could. I was excited to spend time with him and whoever else was at the armory. It was much better than feeling sad about being home alone during the Superbowl and not having easy access to my sister, nieces, and nephew.

Life has a way of connecting people. Mimi and Moncho lived together up until his last breath. I love the bond they shared. They last lived in the Bronx together. When Mimi decided to relocate from Castle Hill to Illinois after Moncho passed, it was bittersweet. We've always been so close. Her children are practically mine. But she moved her family to Illinois, where my brother, Chunky, had settled with my sister (in-law), Amanda, and their kids, Katie and David. Seeking better opportunities. I couldn't have been happier for her and the kiddos. I missed them dearly, as I lived alone in Parkchester in the Bronx, but I was happy for them.

When I moved into my Bronx apartment after my divorce, I was selective about visitors. Just a small circle of trusted friends and family. Serrano took one look at my floors and decided they needed work. I couldn't have cared less about them, but that wasn't Serrano's way. We got permission from the owner, who had lived there with her daughter for years, and Serrano threw himself into the project with enthusiasm. I can still see his short, strong frame manning that huge floor machine, dancing as he worked. The tiny pharmacy speakers he insisted on buying filled the apartment with Frankie Ruiz, Marc Anthony, Tito Nieves, and Hector Lavoe. His loud laugh echoed off those newly finished floors, perfect and proud like everything he touched.

After we got to the 69th Regiment Armory, I settled into a spot at the bar, nursing my beer and watching the game. The place had that comfortable buzz of people cheering, trash-talking, and forgetting about Monday Morning.

These two men in suits walked in.

Who would come to the Armory wearing a suit on a Super Bowl Sunday? I wondered, taking in their formal attire among all our t-shirts, jerseys, jeans, and sweats. Even as I judged them for being overdressed, I had to admit, one of them was attractive.

I leaned over to Serrano. "Who's that?"

"I'll introduce you two," he said, already getting up from his stool.

"Wait! Stop!" I called after him, but he was already walking away. "Where are you going?"

My stomach dropped. Though I loved having fun, I was still shy when it came to meeting new men. *Shit! He's talking to him*, I thought, watching Serrano gesture in my direction. *Act cool. Just act cool.*

The guy I'd been eyeing walked over, and I tried to look casual. Our conversation was short and mostly unmemorable. I learned he was on the clock as an NYPD Homicide Detective. But somehow, by the end of it, we'd exchanged numbers.

It's been twelve years since then, and Jose and I have been married for seven of them.

At the armory, Serrano was our protector, our comic relief, our heart. He would lovingly call us "pendejas" when we got too serious, breaking tension with that loud laugh of his. We'd all be there: Mimi, her coworkers, me and friends. During beer festivals, he would join us, running around the Armory like it was an adult maze. His presence made every moment lighter, more alive. And the Yankees games—those were sacred. We would meet him by the bleachers' food stand, our regular spot for talking trash about the teams while drinking beer and eating overpriced ballpark food. Even now, at that spot in Yankee Stadium, I can feel his presence.

Serrano passed away unexpectedly - too much like Moncho, too sudden, too soon. The funeral service was filled with the family from the armory, and many more. Yet even at his funeral, there was this lightness, this spark of joy that felt so perfectly Serrano. His son was there, of course. Wherever Serrano went, his boy was never far behind. I still think of Serrano with joy when I'm cleaning my apartment, salsa music blasting, or during baseball season. That's the thing about grief—it lives in the music, laughter, and pride of a job well done. Serrano taught me that and I miss him dearly.

The Armory had been part of both mine and Jose's lives long before we ever met. I'd been going there since I was a teenager (my older sister would get me in) while Jose had been connected to it since before he was even born. His father, Pop, was a Vietnam Veteran of the 69th Regiment Infantry. We'd somehow never crossed paths in all those years until that Super Bowl Sunday when Serrano introduced us.

Later, we learned that Serrano and Pop were good friends from the Armory.

And that is how I found myself sitting next to Pop at one of our favorite restaurants, meeting Jose's father for the first time. Jose had been talking about arranging this gathering for weeks, and I could tell it mattered to him. I'd heard enough stories about Pop to know this wasn't going to be casual small talk over dinner.

When Pop walked into the restaurant, I spotted him immediately from the way he carried himself. Everything about him screamed retired military. He had perfect posture, his eyes were assessing the entire restaurant with each measured step he took to us. Jose stood to greet him and then turned to make the introductions.

No small talk. No pleasantries.

"Where's your father from?" he asked, his voice carrying the weight of judgment.

"Morovis," I answered, meeting his gaze.

"Your mother?"

"Santa Isabel. Ponce."

"Did you ever go to the festivals in the summer?"

"Oh, as a teenager we spent plenty of summers enjoying the live music in the Fiesta Patronales."

Something shifted in his face, his shoulders relaxed, and what looked like relief washed over him. Later, I'd learn about his old-school rivalry with Dominicans, something I never quite understood but apparently had just helped me pass some invisible test. He wanted to confirm that I was, in fact, from a Puerto Rican family.

His stern expression softened.

This man, who'd just interrogated me like I was applying for a security clearance, suddenly became someone entirely different. He caught me totally off guard and started to open up completely. Right there, within minutes of meeting me, he began sharing his deepest regrets about not being there for Jose during childhood. His voice carried the weight of years of guilt as he talked about missing so much, about the mistakes he'd made.

"But look at him now," Pop said, his chest filling with unmistakable pride. "Growing up in the Lower East Side during rough times, surrounded by drugs and violence, he chose a different path. He helps people feel safe now and has created financial security for himself."

I sat there, listening to this man I'd just met pour out his heart about his relationship with his son. The vulnerability, the willingness to share such intimate regrets with someone who was essentially a stranger. It felt like the beginning of something important, like he was offering me a piece of himself that would become the foundation of whatever relationship we'd build.

Looking back, that conversation was the first thread in what became a tight bond for us.

His weekly phone calls became a constant in my life. "Yo, it's your father-in-law," he said in a message I have saved on my phone. "Anyway, checking up on you, give me a call." That's Pop—he would start with jokes but always got to the heart: "No, seriously. How are you doing? You good?" His love showed up in actions: the Christmas tradition of him placing the ornament on top of our tree, those check-in calls; and I knew if I were in a ditch, he would be the one to get me out.

I only saw him truly angry or annoyed at me once during the planning of Jose's retirement party, when something about the invitations set him off. But even then, he called back minutes later: "Negrita, you okay? We good?" Of course we were good. I freaking love that man.

Before our wedding in Puerto Rico, Jose and I had a civil ceremony at New York City Hall. I'm not particularly attentive to traditional detail. As we walked toward the ceremony room, Pop glanced at my empty hands and paused. "You don't have flowers," he said, and then he turned to Jose with that firm, fatherly nod: "Go get her flowers." Minutes later, Jose returned with a bouquet of flowers in my favorite color, Yankees (midnight) blue. In that simple gesture, I felt the full weight of Pop's love, the way he noticed the little things and made sure I was treated right.

When the brain cancer came, it moved fast. He had just visited us that summer, beaming with pride at his son and our house, sharing laughs with the family. Even in the hospital, he kept his sense of humor, complaining once more about the nurses waking him up to "clean my balls." I'm sorry for the vulgarity, but that was Pop! That is the version of Pop I knew.

Watching Jose lose him was its own kind of heartbreak. They'd become best friends in Jose's adulthood, rebuilding what was lost in childhood, sharing secrets and bonds that run deep. Pop passed away, and it felt like losing my father all over again. This man who embraced me so completely into his world. But for Jose, it was losing both his dad and his best friend at once. Does anyone ever not feel shattered after losing their father? Their best friend? We all miss Pop, but in Jose's grief, I see the prize and the price of that beautiful second chance they'd built together—the deeper the love, the deeper the loss.

And then there was Archie, who we called Funcle. Jose's uncle by marriage to Titi Linda. When Jose first took me to visit them in New Jersey, he may have introduced me as "just a friend," but Funcle saw right through that. Later he told us, with his knowing smile, "I knew you guys weren't just friends. I could see the connection."

Funcle and Titi Linda's house became a second home when we visited, which says a lot because I'm not usually comfortable staying over at other people's places. But there was something about those weekends in Jersey. The moment you walked in, you would hear Funcle's booming "Familia!" calling everyone for shots, his laughter filling every corner of the house. Funcle would cook his heart out, his steak and guacamole are legendary, rivaled only by Titi Linda's famous buffalo chicken dip (a recipe I have mastered and share with others). There wasn't one game night that stood out because they were all special, each one perfect in its own way.

He wore this T-shirt sometimes that said, "Fucking Shit Up" and that was Funcle in a nutshell. He would speak his mind, share his encyclopedic knowledge about absolutely everything, and do it all with so much love you couldn't help but be drawn in. Politics, his Cuban immigrant experience, the ups and downs of owning his dream restaurant Mi Sueño. He approached every topic with passion and wisdom. Even when we disagreed politically, it never changed how much we loved each other. That was the beauty of Funcle. He created space for you to be entirely yourself.

In a corner of my office stands a bookshelf he built for me, a daily reminder of his craftsmanship and care. I look at it every day, this physical piece of his love that somehow makes his loss feel both harder and easier to bear. As the night wore on and exhaustion set in during those Jersey weekends, I would do something that still makes me smile to think about: I would show up in my pajamas, or change into them early, trying to subtly convince Funcle it was bedtime. Sometimes I would outright beg him to go to sleep so I wouldn't have to be the first one to call it a night.

The way he and Titi Linda interacted made their house feel like home—not because they never disagreed (their debates were hilarious), but because their love made room for everyone's quirks and imperfections. They accepted me completely - the chipper, quirky, clumsy gal they came to love.

I never let myself fully acknowledge his health struggles. Maybe it was denial, maybe self-protection, but his passing shocked me to my core. It still does. But his memory lives on in that Jersey house, in his amazing kids and their big, beautiful families, in every shot of tequila and plate of good food, in that bookshelf that watches over my daily work. In everything I do, really. He's here.

Through all these relationships and losses, I have learned that grief truly is love. Moncho taught me that forgiveness and change are possible and that one precious year of genuine connection can heal decades of pain. His last "Who loves you?" echoes in my heart, answered now not just with "Jesus" but with the deep understanding that love transcends sobriety, addiction, and even death itself.

Serrano showed me how to find joy in the work of living, how to move through life with music in your steps and pride in your heritage. His laughter can still be heard and his presence still lingers in that spot by the Yankee Stadium bleachers, and sometimes the grief shows up in salsa rhythms.

The memory of Pop's weekly calls reminds me that love often speaks in simple phrases: "Yo, it's your father-in-law. Checking up on you." His voicemails I can't bring myself to delete teach me that family isn't just born, it's built through consistent acts of care, through Christmas tree ornaments and flower bouquets, through the kind of honesty that calls just to ask, "You good?" When Jose lost his father and best friend in one person, I understood how second chances at love make the loss both harder and more precious.

And Funcle, whose bookshelf stands in my office, showed me how home isn't a place but a feeling created through late-night conversations, shared meals, and the freedom to be completely yourself. His sudden loss still aches, but his legacy lives in every family gathering, every shot raised with a cry of "¡Familia!"

Father figures come in many forms: in the biological father who thankfully found his way back, in the protector who danced while he worked, in the father-in-law who checked in weekly, in the uncle who saw right through "just friends" and loved me as his own. Their losses left me understanding and accepting that grief had made its home in my heart.

This is why I do the work I do now. Each loss has been a teacher, and grief is messy! In helping others navigate their journeys through loss, I've found purpose.

I miss them all so much.

But love doesn't end with loss.

Each father figure shapes not just how I handle loss, but how I embrace love, right here, right now.

ADJUSTING TO THE PITCH

Players must remain fluid, adapting to whatever pitch gets thrown them.

The fluorescent lights in the Florida Emergency Room felt too bright, making everything seem surreal. I am lying in a hospital bed.

"What you experienced was a TIA. You have a second chance to change your life," the doctor at the Florida Emergency Room repeats to me.

"A what? An auntie? A...*Tia*?" I ask, super confused.

"A transient ischemic attack. A ministroke," replies the doctor in this annoying manner.

"Impossible!" I am in disbelief. "I just ran the New York City Marathon for the second time a little over a week ago. I'm still in my 30s—late 30s, but still. How could this happen?"

The doctor patiently explains all the possibilities before suggesting further testing: stress, family disposition, lack of oxygen to the brain, high blood pressure, cholesterol, poor sleep patterns, impairments of blood vessels, and other health concerns. The list seems endless. As I lie there listening, my thoughts turn to my loved ones and my unexpected journey to becoming a runner.

The memory comes flooding back. Every week, Mami and I took the bus down to Brookdale for my allergy shots. The ride always made me nervous, but I'd grown to enjoy the visits once we got there. My allergist was different from the other doctors. He actually seemed interested in me as a person.

"So, what do you want to do with your life?" he asked during one appointment, settling into his chair as the nurse prepared my injection.

I stood up and walked over to his wall, running my finger

along the frames of his diplomas. "I want to earn a higher education degree like you," I told him. "I want to help people." Then I turned back to face him. "And I want to run track," I said sadly.

His expression grew concerned. "What did the other doctors tell you about running?"

"The inpatient doctor laughed at me," I said, feeling that familiar sting of embarrassment. "He said it was impossible because of my chronic asthma."

My allergist shook his head. "I'm sorry he said that to you. If you really want to help people and also be a runner, you can do it. Don't let anyone tell you otherwise."

I believed him completely. Those words stayed with me, even though I wasn't sure when I'd be able to test them.

I'd never been an athletic person. I loved watching sports, but I didn't have an athletic bone in my body. As an adult, I took classes like cardio kickboxing, yoga, a little CrossFit, and barre. And I did a few mud runs, but that was it.

In 2016, Jose decided to issue me a challenge. He'd already completed a NYC marathon and was always trying to get me to be more active.

"Come on," he said one evening, lacing up his running shoes. "Just run one mile with me. One mile."

Was I excited? Absolutely not. But don't challenge me. "Fine," I said, grabbing my sneakers. "I'll run *one* mile."

Thank goodness I remembered to grab my asthma inhaler. We started off down the street, and within the next few minutes, I was already wondering what I'd gotten myself into. My lungs burned, my legs felt heavy, and that one mile stretched out like it was a full marathon.

But when we finally stopped and I caught my breath, something unexpected happened. The feeling that washed over me was overwhelming. I felt like I could do anything. Like maybe that teenage girl who'd dreamed of running had been waiting to come out all along.

That's how my running journey began.

The discipline it took to prepare for my first marathon was intense. I was working full-time as a Social Worker and Administrator in Health Care while also running my part-time private practice. I had demanding work hours but still managed to get all my runs in. It wasn't easy, though. There were times when I wanted to curse Jose out, and though he never admitted it, I'm sure he felt the same way. I'd often get in my head due to fear and insecurity – what if I had an asthma attack? Was I too slow? Was I fast enough?

What I discovered during that time was that running on my own is therapeutic. It became dedicated time for myself where I could just zone out, listen to music, dive into a podcast, or lose myself in an audiobook. Living a life serving others is my calling and I love it, but I was learning the importance of setting boundaries and having time for myself. Running became an outlet.

We ran throughout all of New York, New Jersey, and Puerto Rico. I joined New York Road Runners. We ran so many different races. I was having a great time, and my body was loving it. It felt stronger with each step, and I was running miles on end. The training was teaching me that success requires showing up every day, regardless of circumstances.

My first half-marathon tested everything in me, but I was too stubborn and determined to quit!

I'd chosen a half-marathon in Brooklyn that had very few water stations. I wore compression socks that were too tight, and the arm brace holding my phone kept slipping off. I felt like I was going to pass out right before the finish line, and I may have even tinkled on myself. But I forgot how awful that felt once I crossed that finish line.

I turned to Jose, who had the biggest grin on his face, and asked, "When's the next one?"

November 2017 came, and I was blessed to have a blast at the NYC marathon. It was truly a 26.2-mile block party through different neighborhoods, starting in Staten Island. I didn't listen to music because the cheers from the crowd were enough to keep me going. I did it and had so much fun! Every step of that journey taught me that discomfort was temporary, but achievement lasts forever.

Now, lying in this hospital bed after a TIA, the reality of all this starts falling into place. My second marathon had been a struggle from start to finish. I'd been juggling two businesses, barely sleeping, constantly stressed. My training had suffered, and deep down, I'd known I wasn't prepared. But I'd pushed through anyway, trying to prove something to myself.

The irony wasn't lost on me that I'd spent years learning discipline through running, and then I'd abandoned that very discipline when life got overwhelming.

As I stared at the ceiling tiles, a thought came to me, clear as day: *Moncho, I love you, but I know I don't need to be reunited with you just yet.*

This ministroke wasn't just a medical event. It was my body telling me it was time to pivot. Time to remember what running had taught me about knowing when to adjust my pace.

By the end of 2022 and start of 2023, I began to make profound changes in my life to ensure I took care of myself. I spent six weeks in New York City to regroup or adjust my pace, as it were. It was the best decision I could have made. I cut back my work hours, learned to refer people out when needed, and I was no longer afraid to say no to others because it meant saying yes to myself.

Having a running injury is never fun, but it gave me the opportunity to apply the lessons I had learned in marathon training: discipline, perseverance, and adaptability. I learned to preserve my energy to avoid burnout and overtraining. These lessons I also applied to my personal life.

In November of 2024, I completed my third marathon, *Every*

Woman's Marathon in Savannah, Georgia. This time, I applied the lessons I worked so hard to relearn. Crossing that finish line felt like more than completing a race. It felt like proof that I had truly learned to listen to my body and honor my limits while still pursuing my goals.

Looking back at those weekly trips to Brookdale with my mom, at that young girl who dreamed of running despite her asthma, I can see how far I've come. My recent achievements as a runner are a testament to that, and because there's always another race, I look forward to how far I can still go.

REHABBING

Injuries—physical, mental, emotional—need rehabilitation to be ready for the next season/game.

Have you ever had one of those moments where everything in your life seems to line up with a random sports event? No? Maybe? It can't be just me. Picture this: It was July 9th, 2011, and I was sitting on the living room floor, surrounded by boxes I had yet to unpack since moving in a few weeks before. I was watching the Yankees face Tampa Bay Rays on TV when Derek Jeter stepped up to the plate at Yankee Stadium.

Just weeks before, I separated from my ex-husband. Talk about a curveball. I felt relieved and devastated all at once. I had so many conflicting emotions. But the end of our marriage felt like a milestone.

When Jeter's bat connected with the ball, the crowd erupted. His 3,000th hit! A true milestone. The House that Derek Built went absolutely wild, and I found myself jumping up, cheering at the TV like I was right there in the stands.

Then I sat back down and started crying.

Not because of baseball, though watching Jeter achieve that milestone was moving. I was crying because everything felt so contradictory. Here was the moment of triumph on the screen, while my own life felt like I'd just struck out in the bottom of the ninth yet still won a World Series championship.

I was relieved and devastated all at once. Proud and ashamed. Free and terrified. I remember catching my reflection in the TV screen during a commercial break. I was smiling and crying at the same time. It wasn't a pretty look.

The end of my marriage felt like a personal milestone, too, but my emotional state was far more complex than pure happiness or excitement. One moment, I felt confident about my decision, and the next I was drowning in doubt and anxiety.

I knew ending the relationship had been the best decision for both of us, yet I couldn't stop replaying every moment, every fight, every missed connection. Where had I gone wrong? It was like reviewing game footage over and over, analyzing every plan and every decision, searching for that error that cost us the game.

I attended my ten-year high school reunion at Brandeis High School that same year. My soul needed that experience, with meaningful connections and a sense of continuity when I needed it most. There were hugs, memories, laughter and loving banter.

Even as I laughed and caught up with classmates, I was also navigating the turbulent waters of grief. It was then that I decided to start therapy. It was the beginning of my self-discovery and healing journeys.

In the quiet moments between reunions with friends and baseball games, doubt crept in. I found myself questioning past decisions, wondering if breaking up with my first boyfriend was my own personal strikeout. The what ifs played on a loop in my mind, a highlight reel of missed opportunities and second guesses.

Truth be told, those what ifs weren't just about past relationships. They were inextricably tied to a deeper, more profound loss. When Moncho passed away, his absence left a gaping hole in my life. I knew that he didn't approve of my ex-husband, but he favored my first boyfriend. Was that what I was missing? Was I longing for the connections that Moncho had fostered with others?

Let's not get it twisted—I'm not idolizing anyone here. But the reality was I truly missed my dad. This led me to appreciate the relationships he had with other people. I missed Moncho (and I still do). I missed his guidance, his perspective, even his disapproval; all of it. It was like trying to play a crucial game without my coach in the dugout.

But I was also trying to hide the anger I was feeling.

Initially, I found myself blaming my parents. I've never been comfortable with anger, preferring to maintain a calm exterior like a seasoned player unfazed by a tough call. But the anger was there, bubbling beneath the surface. I was angry and hurt by the experiences we had to endure growing up—the substance abuse, the domestic violence, and other traumas. These were heavy burdens to carry onto the field of adult life.

At twenty-one, I'd talked about marriage as if it was just another base to touch on the way to home plate. Why hadn't my parents warned me? Why didn't they call a time-out on my hasty decision?

Walking into that first session felt like stepping into a trainer's room after a serious injury. I was hurting, and I needed professional help to heal properly.

"What brings you here today?" my therapist asked, settling into her chair across from me.

I took a deep breath. "My marriage is over, my dad is dead, and I don't know who I am anymore."

It wasn't elegant, but it was honest.

Processing my anger was like going through injury rehabilitation. It was painful but necessary. Each therapy session was another step in my recovery, helping me understand that my emotional injuries needed as much attention as any physical wound would.

In therapy, I began unpacking not just the obvious traumas – the addiction, the violence, the instability, but also the quieter wounds. The time in fourth grade when an adult stranger violated my trust and my body, leaving me to carry that secret alone to protect my mother's fragile health. I'd learned to disconnect during that experience, a coping mechanism that served me in childhood but needed examining in adulthood. Like my anger toward my parents, this too required gentle rehabilitation and learning to reconnect with part of myself I'd learned to shut down.

But just as quickly as this anger flared, it subsided. Holding onto it felt like gripping the bat too tightly, restricting my swing. I developed deep compassion for my parents. They'd done the best they could while also navigating their own traumas. With the wisdom of hindsight and therapy, I began to understand that anger, like any emotion, wasn't bad. Growing up seeing the adults around me have outbursts when angry or hurt made me think of anger as a villain. But it wasn't. It was what I did with that anger that mattered.

Living alone for the first time was like stepping up to bat in a crucial game. The silence of an empty apartment could be deafening, filled with the echoes of the life I had left behind. But gradually, that silence became a canvas for self-discovery.

I remember having a few friends over for Christmas that year. I didn't have the energy or time to buy a real tree, so I created a Christmas tree on my wall with packing tape, arranging it in the shape of a Christmas tree and hanging ornaments from the tape. My friends and I thought it was the cutest thing ever.

"Only you would turn packing tape into Christmas magic," Nancy laughed when I sent her the picture. She was right. I'd never needed much to feel happy. Just love and peace.

Another time, Ely and I attempted to put together a kitchen table I'd bought. I say "we," but she probably did all the work. I'm not handy, though I try. At that time, I was working two jobs with pretty low salaries, even though they were in my career field. I could write a book on underpaid social workers, but I digress.

As I focused on rebuilding my career, I realized that taking time for myself was necessary. It was my turn at bat, and I needed to step up to the plate with all the strength and focus I could muster.

I was determined to play this inning of my life with everything I had. I studied and earned my clinical license in social work. A friend gave me a ride on the morning of my licensing exam so I wouldn't have to worry about train delays. Then, Nancy and I celebrated at the seaport after I finished.

When Jeter's 2012 and 2013 seasons were cut short by injury,

I watched him take time from the game to heal and recover. In my life, I did the same. Depression, anxiety, and partying too much weren't healthy coping mechanisms. Therapy became my training room, and in that safe space, I was able to start truly accepting things that happened in the past for what they were and working through feelings of anger, hurt, confusion, and shame.

I continued to surround myself with people who truly loved me and whom I loved. People who were healthy and didn't have toxic ways of being.

Looking back now, I see those years not just as a time of recovery but as a season of growth. I was working on myself and appreciating my new life. I have no regrets about past decisions. They all led to where I am and that brings me tremendous joy.

I started a new position in health care, and that salary allowed me to work just one full-time position while opening my part-time private practice in NYC—right across from the Empire State Building. I take great pride in myself because I never give up. Even through past breakups, I know I made the right decisions for myself.

I still had some anger, though, especially toward Moncho. I wished I had him physically there to tell me it would be okay, that I would be okay through the early years of my childhood and even as an adult. But I also came to appreciate time I did have with him, even if it wasn't enough, even if it wasn't perfect.

In baseball, as in life, there are no guarantees. But with every swing, every step, and every breath, we have the chance to create something beautiful. And that is a reason to keep playing, keep hoping, and keep appreciating every moment of this unpredictable game we call life, even when we're missing our most cherished coaches.

Swinging with a Purpose

When a batter stands at the plate to strategically hit
the ball toward specific spots on the field
or hit a home run.

There they were: two pink lines that would change everything. Like a batter stepping up to the plate, I thought I knew exactly where this pitch was heading. I was shocked and scared, and I made an appointment with my gynecologist as soon as I found out.

Are these tests correct? I took two to make sure, but I still was not sure.

Two lines. Definitely two lines.

I went midday to my gynecologist's office, and they did a sonogram.

Two pink lines again.

The sound of the heartbeat filled my heart, and somehow, I was already in love with that tiny possibility growing inside of me.

Suddenly, I wasn't just a therapist, wife, sister, or friend. I was becoming a mother. I started daydreaming about all the possibilities with this tiny human filled with pure joy. I caught myself smiling mid-conversation in meetings or while talking to anyone.

Then came March 2020.

We'd just returned from a weekend in Philadelphia celebrating our wedding anniversary. I'd been spotting during the trip, which made me nervous, but when I called the doctor's office, they told me I didn't need to seek immediate medical treatment since I already had an appointment scheduled for Monday.

Jose and I walked into the ultrasound room together, and

the tech was just as chipper as I was. "Let's see how baby's doing," she said, squeezing the cold gel onto my belly.

I watched her face as she moved the wand around, looking for that familiar heartbeat we'd heard before. But her expression began to change.

Then there was silence.

I couldn't see the ultrasound and I could feel a stillness in the room that sent chills through my body.

"Is everything okay?" I asked, my voice barely above a whisper.

"I'll get the doctor for you," she said and walked away before I could ask anything else.

Jose and I sat there in that empty room, the silence deafening. I knew. Somehow, I already knew.

We were moved to another office where our doctor sat across from us, her expression gentle but serious. "I'm sorry," she began. "You've miscarried."

The words hit like a pitch I never saw coming.

She kept talking about how one out of four pregnancies end in miscarriage, how common it was, how it wasn't anything we did. But statistics offered no comfort when grief was already settling into my chest like a weight I'd never be able to lift.

I couldn't hear what she was saying anymore. Everything was muffled.

Later, I reached out to my regular gynecologist, the one I'd been seeing for years who felt like family. He sat me and Jose down in his office, looked us both in the eyes, and validated our feelings.

"This isn't your fault," he said firmly. "Nothing you did or didn't do caused this."

I felt empty. Literally empty!

He explained what would happen physically in the next couple of days, trying to prepare us for what he called "the worst natural process." In a sense, he did prepare me, but nothing could have prepared me for the emotional devastation that followed.

It happened just as he said it would. The physical pain was immense, and the bleeding seemed to go on forever. My sister, brother-in-law, niece, and nephew were staying with us for support, but I kept running to the bathroom, trying to hide the worst of it from them.

This deep sadness and emptiness crept further into me with every breath I took.

It happened on a Sunday. When I got a text message from an administrator saying that I had to cover healthcare sites the following day. I explained my situation

"This is common," said their reply, as if I should just get over it and show up to work.

I was devastated. There was a future that would never be.

I was working in healthcare during the peak of the COVID pandemic. The world around us was in chaos – racial injustice, police brutality, a political climate dividing communities. There was fear and isolation and so much death everywhere I looked.

I kept working from home because I was too depressed to go into the office in person. I worked in the same pajamas for days at a time, not caring about anything beyond getting through each Zoom call.

My grief found its way into every little crevice of my life. The baby apps I'd downloaded kept sending me updates about how big my baby should be getting. I had to throw away the maternity clothes I'd already started buying. I tried to go on runs but would break down when I saw mothers walking in the neighborhood with their strollers.

I had to shake this off, I told myself. I filled every hour with client sessions, paperwork, and continuing education. Anything to keep my mind busy and my heart from feeling.

But grief always crept in.

One day, I found myself sobbing inside a pizza shop because I saw a pregnant woman ordering a slice. I sat there in that bright-lit restaurant, surrounded by families and the smell of melted cheese, realizing I couldn't hide from this pain forever.

My decision to leave healthcare wasn't easy. I knew the

positive impact I was making in communities, but I couldn't stomach (funny, using that word) another Zoom call or make sense of the numbers on the endless Excel spreadsheets. I still had my part-time private practice, though.

We were living in a tiny one-bedroom apartment in the Bronx. I took my video sessions with my clients using a fold-up chair and table, positioning myself with my back against the window curtains so they wouldn't see into our bedroom. All the while, Jose stayed in the living room until the late evening hours when I would finally be done for the day.

It took a while, but I was finally finding joy and purpose, providing mental health services during this chaotic time.

Jose and Nancy were my biggest supporters, encouraging me to go full-time in my private practice.

"What if I fail?" I asked Jose one evening as we sat on our tiny couch.

He looked at me with this steady confidence and said, "We'll figure it out."

"What if I don't have enough clients?"

Nancy reassured me: "If you build it, they will come." (If you haven't watched *Field of Dreams*, you should.) Nancy had always had this trust and belief in me since we met working at a domestic violence shelter and discovered we were both Yankee fans who'd attended the same graduate school.

I submit my resignation, and in May 2020, I traded working in healthcare for my own entirely virtual mental health practice.

My first week as a full-time entrepreneur, I woke up anxiously checking my phone for cancelations. But my clients came. They stayed. They committed to themselves and their healing. Their trust in me helped me begin to trust myself again. It was like learning to swing again after a devastating strikeout. Each client session, each small victory, was another chance to step up to the plate.

While my career was sorting itself out, I was still trying to feel at home with my changed body and life. We moved to

Florida and were ecstatic about the fresh start! My practice grew faster than I expected, but so did the weight of my grief.

I gained so many pounds that people started commenting. "I didn't think you could even gain weight," someone said, as if my naturally thin frame was some kind of superpower that grief couldn't touch.

But it could, and it did. I was eating my emotions, barely getting any exercise in, and working from home meant no commute to force movement into my day. I was straying from who I used to be.

Losing my baby made me question everything I knew about healing for myself. It was so much easier to help others in their healing journey. But now it was time to invest in myself.

I started small. I bought new running sneakers, increased my therapy sessions, began tapping into unresolved childhood trauma, and committed to being honest about how I was feeling to myself and others.

Having a good work ethic has always been my jam, but I couldn't outwork my grief. I knew I needed to balance my work with actually taking care of myself, so I collaborated with an amazing online business manager whose name was, coincidently, Jessica.

In a relatively short time and through lots of dedicated hours, days, and nights, we were able to self-publish *My Self-Healing Journal*, a self-guided interactive journal to help others start their healing journey.

When I received the approval from the Library of Congress, I cried. It was heartwarming to think about how my life experiences had all led to and informed the work I was doing helping others.

Over time, I was able to accept my miscarriage and even appreciate that time in my life. Now, I also appreciate my decision not to have any children of my own. I have amazing nieces, nephews, and godchildren. It isn't a desire or need in my life anymore. I do have a French bulldog named Mugzy, and being a dog mom fulfills me in ways I never expected.

My practice is filled with radiant souls who trust me with their stories and are committed to their healing.

Healing doesn't mean forgetting, ignoring, or masking your pain with hours of work. It means making room for all of it. It's messy, with conflicting emotions, but there's also growth. Some mornings I think about how old my baby would be. Some mornings I'm excited about gathering with my grief group. Some mornings I'm so excited to be responsible for no one except myself and Mugzy. All kinds of mornings and feelings are valid and part of who I am now.

As I write this essay, I'm gazing over at the last sonogram photo on my alter.

"Thank you," I say quietly. "You changed me."

I find a new way to be whole.

THE WALKOFF

**When the home team is at bat in the bottom
of the 9th inning with the score tied or losing,
and they score enough runs to walk off the field victo-
riously with the win.**

When Derek Jeter announces his final season with the New York Yankees in 2014, it marks more than just the end of an era in baseball. For me, it becomes a catalyst for reflection, growth, and a newfound appreciation for life's journey. I feel an overwhelming excitement and nostalgia.

As a kid, Moncho whisked us away to softball games on the weekends, when he and my uncles played. They say it all starts with family, indeed, my love for baseball is seeded within mine. It was a game that bound us together. Uncles and aunts joined the chorus of cheering, booing, shouting, and cursing, regardless of if we won or lost. We were all players and spectators in our own right.

With excitement rushing through me, I watched as Moncho parked the car at the field's parking lot. Moncho's tall stature exuded a powerful presence, and his friendly waves to others made it seem like he knew everyone around. He had a knack for bringing smiles and laughter to those he interacted with.

The victories led us to bars for celebratory gatherings, and losses were met with camaraderie and reflection. We always celebrated - win or lose. In those early days, I learned to honor both the small and grand triumphs.

But like all seasons, this one, too, ends. Moncho stopped playing softball.

The cherished moments with my paternal family slipped away, leaving me optimistically longing for a return. Was it softball I longed for? Was it Moncho?

He was struggling with substance abuse.

I started watching baseball.

Old Timers' Day, a day when MLB teams honor retired players, is especially memorable in 2014. Yogi Berra, Whitey Ford, Rickey Henderson, Reggie Jackson, Joe Torre, Hideki Matsui, David Cone, Joe Girardi, Tino Martinez, and so many more are in attendance. It transports me back to my teenage years, attending games with Ely and other friends. Those good years in high school and undergraduate studies flood back to me. There is a bittersweetness to it all. I have lost precious years with them. But when we reconnected years prior, the love and bonds were still there, unchanged. Still are.

In 2014, Nancy and I become season ticket holders, determined to witness as much of Jeter's farewell tour as possible. We are on a mission. We go to numerous games, even venturing into enemy territory at Boston's Fenway Park. I feel the chill at Fenway and the respect for the rivalry—the Yankees and Derek Jeter. My sister is getting married that day, but nope, not missing Jeter's final game at Fenway. (Don't worry - even though I don't know this at the time, she and her partner aren't going to stay together, so no love lost.)

The peak of this emotional season comes during Jeter's final game at Yankee Stadium. I am there with Nancy and other friends, sharing this historic moment with the ones who understand its significance. Our seats are in the 400 level (the nosebleeds), but we don't care. Truthfully, it doesn't matter. We are in the house, though we joke around about being so close to Papa Dios!

As Jeter approaches the plate with his trademark confidence and swagger, the air is electric. The crack of the bat and the roar of the crowd stops time for me. His walk-off hit seals the Yankees' win and provides an epic ending to his career in the Bronx.

In that moment, a flood of memories rush through me. I am transported back to when my parents were just teens and young adults. I can almost see my mother's determination, feel the weight of my father's substance abuse struggles, and taste the highlights of my life. My mind and heart wander to my parents' young love derailed by drugs and domestic violence, my mother's fierce dedication to staying healthy and to her daughters, and my father's enduring love despite his struggles with substance abuse. I remember the challenges of my own past, the various experiences that have shaped me, from witnessing domestic violence, rape, and substance abuse to building meaningful relationships, especially during my preteen and teen years, to feeling the deep pain of my father's death. I think about how I opened my solo private practice in the penthouse of 19 West 34th Street, right across the street from The Empire State Building. It is a monumental achievement for a city girl who dared to dream big while still living in the Bronx and Brooklyn.

Baseball, particularly the Yankees, has been a constant through it all. The game teaches me about resilience, teamwork, and the beauty of striving for greatness. Jeter embodies these qualities, and his farewell tour becomes a metaphor for embracing life's transitions.

As I sit in the stadium that night with Nancy and friends, I feel a profound sense of gratitude. Gratitude for my parents, who show me love and embody strength in their own ways. Gratitude for the friends and family who stand by me through thick and thin. Gratitude for the lessons learned from both triumphs and mistakes. Gratitude for the wins and losses. And gratitude for the game that has given me so much joy. Legacies are built over time, and that night, not only does Derek Jeter solidify his legacy but I start to become aware of what mine is.

The tears are streaming down my cheeks as I go home. It is never just about baseball. I've watched Derek Jeter play shortstop for the Yankees since I was a teenager, and his consistency was an anchor for when big change was happening in my life. Yes, here I am, watching another chapter close. The grief feels so familiar like when Moncho passed away, when I lost my childhood innocence, when life forces me to say goodbye before I am ready.

Who will be our new shortstop? The question is deeper than that. It is about who *I* am becoming in a world that keeps changing. Moncho taught me that endings are painful, but they make space for new beginnings. He never got to see me become a therapist or open my practice, but his journey in life and his love helps shape the person I continue to grow into. As I watch Jeter play on the field, I feel that dance with grief and hope that comes with all transitions. It's a bittersweet understanding that while nothing lasts forever, each ending carries something new.

Dear Moncho

Dear Moncho,

Do you remember how spoiled I felt in the '90s being a Yankees fan? That feeling was largely attributed to having the greatest closer in baseball history, Mariano Rivera, our beloved Mo. He made it look effortless, didn't he? The way he'd walk onto the mound to "Enter Sandman," the crowd roaring with excitement. Remember how we'd get goosebumps watching him approach the mound to those thundering chords? Those moments were magical.

Mo taught me that endings could be beautiful because they meant another game was on the horizon. Even when he occasionally lost (though it was rare), I found myself looking forward to the next game. There would always be another chance, even if it meant waiting for a new season.

As I write this book of essays about your legacy of love and my relationship with grief, I knew Mariano had to be part of my closing chapter. Not just because he was the GOAT, but because he inadvertently taught me about grief through the game we both loved so much.

Losing you, Moncho, didn't feel that heavy at first, because I prioritized my sister's grief over my own. When I finally allowed myself to lean into my personal sorrow, it hit differently. Some days, it feels like I'm facing Mariano's legendary cutter in the bottom of the ninth, and I strike out, feeling overwhelmed by a whirlwind of anger, sadness, and compassion. Other times, I'm Mo himself, throwing that perfect pitch to clinch the World Series victory. The emotions are as unpredictable as a knuckleball.

I've studied death and dying since my teenage years, but until you experience personal grief, you can't truly comprehend its depth. Moncho, I probably shouldn't have witnessed or experienced some of the things I did growing up. Yet here I am, still standing on the mound. You also endured more than anyone should, and my heart overflows with compassion for your journey.

Mariano reminds me that tomorrow brings another day, another game, another opportunity to honor you through how I play, how I live my life. Endings, even the painful ones, can be faced with grace. I choose to live with intention, knowing that joy and peace will come, just as Mo showed up to each game ready to close it out, come what may.

We've always connected through baseball, and you've shown me that the best way to honor those we've lost is to keep playing, keep showing up for family, friends, and community. Even in the bottom of the ninth, with our hearts on the line, we've got what it takes to get that final out. To me, that means continuing to spread your legacy of love.

As Yogi Berra wisely said, "It ain't over till it's over." And even then, there's always tomorrow's game.

With tons of love and gratitude,
Your lost daughter,
Jess

Author Bio

Jessica Rios is a trauma-informed Psychotherapist, writer, advocate for women and human rights, and a sister, friend, wife, dog mom, and lifelong Yankees fan. Her work with grief began as a teenager at the New York Department for the Aging and continued through her clinical training as a trauma-informed psychotherapist and death doula. Known throughout her career as "the grief therapist," Jess now focuses her private practice on supporting individuals navigating trauma, loss, transitions, and complicated grief.

A native New Yorker, Jess has been devoted to the Yankees since the 1994 season. What began as an escape from the uncertainties of childhood became a lifelong love affair with baseball - one rooted in resilience, ritual, and the belief that even after loss, there is always another at bat.

Acknowledgements

Writing has always been a powerful and therapeutic tool for me. It's a way to process my thoughts, feelings, and lived experiences. Creating this book was a true labor of love. Returning to these moments stirred up feelings of joy, hope, frustration, and optimism. Every part of it was worth it.

Baseball has taught me that patience, strategy, and teamwork matter, and we are never meant to do this alone. We need one another to keep showing up, healing, and thriving. For that, I am deeply grateful to:

My husband, Jose, who encouraged me to get these words onto the paper, especially during the long hours of writing, reflecting, and doubting myself as I revisited some of the harder moments. Thank you for your constant love and support. You reminded me that this didn't need to be perfect to be meaningful, and you helped me make it better in countless ways. I wouldn't change a single thing about our journey together. Now, can we go for wings, tacos, and a beer? Thanks for being such an incredible pawrent to our Mugzy. I love you.

To my sisters: we may remember things differently, and we may have lived through different versions of the same moments, but neither is more valid than the other. I'm sorry for the pain you've carried, and I love you deeply. My life would not be whole without you. My greatest hope is that you always find joy, peace, and lots of laughter. Never let anyone dim your light. Thank you for the love you pour into my nieces and nephews.

To my parents, grandparents, aunts, uncles, and cousins. Thank you for the love, memories, and traditions that shaped who I am.

To my chosen families: the Perez familia, the Vicentes,

Ahmeds, 69th Armory crew, Pitres and Sampers – thank you for your love, support and giving me a sense of home throughout the years.

I have been incredibly blessed to build meaningful friendships, especially with girlfriends who sat with me through the joyful and the messy parts of life. A heartfelt thank you and shout out to my girlfriends from Lettice, Michelle, Shree, Atiya, Elisa, Elizabeth, Noelia, Marsha, Yenely, Massiel, Christine, Debbie, Erika, Julissa, Yesenia, Janely, Melissa, Lorraine, Soraya, Dimitra, Rena, Nancy - thank you for your honesty, accountability, and for showing up consistently while challenging each other to grow while loving me through it all! I'm fortunate to know a group of bright, badass ladies!

Sabrina, my Sabs, when we met in 2020, I knew we were going to work together but I had no idea to what extent. Just a few years later, we were in Chicago reviewing our manuscript. Thank you for believing in me, for your patience, brilliance, and dedication to this labor of love. You understood the mess in my head and we did this! Also, thanks for saying his (Moncho) name. It made my heart smile.

Kerry and Brittany, thank you for taking the time to share your author experiences and for introducing me to Amy. Amy, thank you for believing in this project and for your honesty with every word in this book. I am deeply grateful to the St. Petersburg Publishing team for their support.

Cynthia, thank you for guiding me over these past few years with such wisdom and warmth. It is an honor to have you write the foreword for this book. I am so grateful to share this journey with you on this earth.

To my beta readers and to everyone who took time from their busy lives to read my manuscript and provide (brutally) honest feedback, thank you. And to all who encouraged me to keep writing, you helped get this book onto shelves.

To everyone I've shared Yankee games and baseball moments with, especially my Opening Day crew at the Yankee Tavern, I cherish every memory. Baseball is more than a sport.

It is shared love, connection, and moments that will live with me always.

If you've lost someone you love or if your life didn't turn out the way you thought it would, keep going. Take it one pitch, one at-bat, one inning, one game, one season at a time.

And finally…to the New York Yankees, can we secure #28 already?…PLEASE!